Dear Reader,

Health information often focuses on diseases. It answers questions like "how do you keep from getting cancer?" or "what's the best way to treat arthritis?" But if you look at what characterizes good health as you age, it's not just avoiding conditions like these. It's whether you are strong and capable, and whether you can continue to do all the activities you've done in the past. Can you move easily and without pain? Can you remain independent and self-sufficient? Can you stay in your home, or will you need to move to assisted living or a nursing home?

These are questions that concern everyone, whether or not they are dealing with potentially debilitating health problems. Maintaining your mobility and safeguarding your independence are key goals as you age. Problems with mobility—such as slowed walking or difficulty rising out of a chair—are often the first signs of a decline in health and day-to-day function.

Many people don't think about mobility until they are in their 60s, 70s, and beyond. But working to maintain it really should begin decades earlier. Many of the health problems that come with aging could be avoided or lessened by following healthy habits throughout adulthood. In addition, practices like exercising, building muscle strength, following a balanced diet, and maintaining a healthy weight are all easier if you start in your 40s and 50s. But even if you are older or are already have trouble getting around, simple steps toward better health and physical conditioning can improve your abilities and help prevent further loss of movement.

The goal of this Special Health Report is to do just that. This report will show you how mobility relies on many body systems working together: your bones, muscles, and joints; your senses, brain, and balance system. It will help you understand some of the common changes and health conditions brought on by aging that cause people to begin losing their ability to move. The report translates clinical and scientific knowledge about mobility into practical steps you can take to stay healthy and strong. It takes a broad view of mobility, looking not just at whether you can climb several flights of stairs, but also whether you can move easily around your home and neighborhood, stay connected to your loved ones, and remain engaged in the world. Perhaps most important, this report will encourage you to challenge your body with regular physical activity and exercises that have been shown to preserve or improve mobility.

Whatever your age or health status, now is the time to ensure an active and capable future.

Sincerely,

Scott D. Martin, M.D.
Medical Editor

Harvard Health Publications | Harvard Medical School | 10 Shattuck Street, Second Floor | Boston, MA 02115

Mobility and quality of life

Mobility is the kind of thing you take for granted until you no longer have it. When you're young and healthy, you never stop to consider how marvelous it is to be able to move effortlessly. You get out of bed in the morning, take a shower, then head downstairs to your kitchen to make coffee. You go for your daily walk around the neighborhood, or, if you live in an urban area, you may walk to the post office, library, or gym. Later, you drive across town to meet a good friend for lunch. On the way home you stop at the grocery store, pick up a few things you need for dinner, then carry the bags back to the car and drive home.

Even the simple, relatively uneventful day described here requires a great deal of physical stamina, strength, balance, coordination, and range of motion. It requires the ability to get out of bed easily, take a shower, manage a flight of stairs, walk a quarter or half-mile easily, get in and out of a car, navigate traffic, and carry bags for a fair distance. Most of us spend our lives doing these very tasks day in and day out without marveling at how much our bodies can do. But when we lose these basic skills because of a health problem or the physical decline associated with aging, we begin to understand how much living well relies on being able to move.

Maybe you're relatively young, and joint replacement surgery or physical therapy for an injury is all you need to get you back on your feet. This report will address issues like those. It will also address the deeper, more entrenched problems that come in older age, because, increasingly, there are effective ways of coping—whether with canes and high-tech wheelchairs or with a wide variety of services that can help keep you living on your own.

In addition, this report will look at things you should be doing at every stage of life to promote your health, because ultimately, those, too, play a role in how well you age and therefore how mobile you remain. These include measures such as the following:

- taking care of the joints you need for walking—specifically, hips, knees, and ankles
- caring for your back and posture
- maintaining muscle strength and power
- building your sense of balance to avoid falls
- strengthening core muscles for better stability
- protecting your eyes and ears, and keeping your brain sharp
- maintaining a healthy weight and eating a nutrient-rich diet
- ensuring that your home and environment help rather than hinder your mobility.

These measures can all add up to a healthier future—and greater mobility and independence.

The importance of mobility

Mobility is defined as your ability to move purposefully around your environment. Limitations on mobility affect one-third to one-half of adults ages 65 and older. At first, an impairment might not seem like a big deal—you learn to move slower and more deliberately, or you work around the problem by relying on a cane or walker. But this can lead to a spiral of poor health. As you move less, you may gain weight, stop exercising, and withdraw from social relationships and activities that challenge you mentally. Not exercising can make many health conditions worsen. The resulting physical, emotional, and mental decline further restricts your mobility.

Mobility problems are linked with lower quality of life and higher rates of depression. Over time, these limitations raise your risk of becoming disabled—unable to perform daily activities because of a physical or mental impairment. That's why it's important to intervene to either prevent future mobility impairments or reduce existing ones.

Most important, mobility issues can lead to a loss of independence and can make it impossible for you to live on your own. Even if technology allows you to overcome a lot of challenges, for most people, the ability to rely on their own bodies, skills, and mental agility is a crucial part of living a satisfying life. Mobility allows you to have fulfilling social relationships and to fully engage with the world. It gives you a sense of self-sufficiency. Most people would rather have the capacity to do all the simple acts described earlier than rely on caretakers and assistive devices.

Thinkstock

Measuring mobility

Do you have trouble walking a quarter of a mile? Can you climb stairs on your own and accomplish basic daily tasks like cooking, showering, and going to the grocery store? These are the kinds of questions that clinicians ask when trying to assess mobility limitations. Here are some other factors a doctor, nurse, or physical therapist might use to assess mobility.

Gait. Human walking requires a series of movements: lifting the foot, placing it on the ground ahead of you, and shifting your weight from the heel to the ball of the foot. The way you walk is called your gait. Changes in the speed or pattern of your gait can give your doctor an indication of mobility trouble. Gait often changes with age: healthy people in their 70s generally have a 10% to 20% reduction in the speed of their gait and the length of their stride compared with healthy people in their 20s. There are often other, subtler changes as well—such as using less force when you push off or stooping more when you walk. A more cautious, shuffling gait may be the result of compensating for problems with vision and hearing or bones and muscles. Arthritis often makes people adopt a flat-footed gait, and a bent posture significantly alters walking patterns as the body shifts its center of gravity forward.

Chronic pain and a host of medical conditions can also cause gait abnormalities. Over time, gait changes can weaken or imbalance the muscles you use to walk,

compounding health problems. To assess your gait, a doctor or physical therapist might have you walk about 10 feet across a room while timing you; managing the walk relatively quickly is a sign of good health. An uneven, halting, or shuffling gait is often a sign of an underlying health problem.

The "get up and go" test. Another common test is to have you sit in a chair, and when prompted, rise up and walk about 10 feet in a line, then turn and come back to the chair and sit down. Most people with normal mobility can complete the task in 10 seconds or less. How you accomplish it can also indicate if you have muscle weakness, posture or balance problems, or joint pain.

Simple tasks. A mobility assessment will also focus on how you handle simple tasks and challenges, like stepping over objects on the floor, balancing on one leg, balancing on both feet positioned one in front of the other, and rising from a chair and sitting down several times in a row.

Daily activities. One of the best clues to your mobility is how well you accomplish small daily tasks like bathing, preparing meals, cleaning the house, and going shopping. Many people who have trouble moving still do these tasks, but they may change the way they do them—sitting on a chair in the shower, for instance.

Range of travel. There's a difference between what people *can* do and what they *actually* do. Mobility researchers have developed tools like the Life-Space Assessment, which looks at the area through which people travel in their daily routine as a way of representing their actual mobility in daily life. The advantage of such a tool is that it takes into account real-world adaptations you use to boost your mobility (for example, using a cane or wheelchair, or driving and using public transportation) as well as nonphysical factors that affect mobility (such as depression, lack of motivation, or lack of financial resources).

Improving your mobility

A fundamental goal of healthy aging is to keep walking as long as possible. Barring an injury or disabling disease, most of us think of the ability to walk as a defining capability of the human body. Of course, people who lose their ability to walk can still retain mobility through wheelchairs and assistive devices, and they can have full and happy lives. But there's no reason why most people can't keep walking their whole lives. It's important to stay active in order to maintain this ability—or, if you haven't been active for a while, to start with whatever simple measures it takes to boost your level of activity.

It can't be emphasized enough: engaging in physical activity is the single most important thing you can do to maintain mobility and independence, no matter your age or your health status. It can help you control your weight—whether that means to avoid putting on pounds or to lose extra weight you already have. It's the key to keeping your muscles and bones strong, your joints working properly, your heart healthy, and your metabolism revved. The more you move, the better your strength and balance will be, and the less likely you will fall or lose the ability to perform basic daily functions like climbing stairs or standing up easily. And that's on top of all the other health benefits of regular exercise, such as reduced risks of cardiovascular disease, type 2 diabetes, metabolic syndrome, and some cancers. Exercise even has positive effects on mood and may help improve cognitive function.

In addition to doing targeted exercises for muscle strength and flexibility, joint health, and balance as described elsewhere in this report, you should strive to increase routine daily physical activities that don't even count as exercise, such as climbing stairs. If you're in pain, all this activity may seem impossible. But in many cases, exercise can actually help you feel better. If you have osteoarthritis, for example, regular exercise not only helps maintain joint function, but also relieves stiffness and decreases pain and fatigue.

How much exercise do you need? For healthy adults, the Physical Activity Guidelines for Americans from the U.S. Department of Health and Human Services recommend 30 minutes of moderate exercise a day, five days a week—or a total of 150 minutes a week. The guidelines also recommend twice-weekly strength training sessions and balance exercises for older adults at risk of falling. Disability should not be a reason to refrain from all activity. The guidelines state: "When older adults cannot do 150 minutes of moderate-intensity aerobic activity a week because of chronic conditions, they should be as physically active as their abilities and conditions allow."

So what should you do? If your joints are the problem, don't try to "pace" your joints—let your joints pace you. For example, don't make yourself go jogging. Instead, pick low-impact activities, such as swimming or water aerobics. Try cycling on a stationary bike at the gym. Yoga, tai chi, and qigong are other good alternatives. Even a gentle walking program that ramps up slowly will help. In other words, there's a lot of flexibility in the kinds of activities you do and when; the key is finding out what works for you. Don't feel guilty if you can't do the same kinds of activities you used to. Establishing a regular, consistent routine is far more helpful than the occasional ambitious workout. The important thing is not to let joint pain keep you from being physically active.

If you're in doubt about your ability to take on an exercise program, we recommend using the Physical Activity Readiness Questionnaire for Everyone (PAR-Q+), a tool developed by the Canadian Society for Exercise Physiology, to help you determine whether you should talk to your doctor before embarking on, or ramping up, an exercise program. You can find it at www.health.harvard.edu/PAR-Q. Whether or not you use the PAR-Q+, we recommend talking to a doctor about whether it's safe to exercise if any of the following applies:

- You've had hip or knee surgery.
- You've been experiencing pain in your hip, knee, or back.
- You have a chronic or unstable health condition, such as heart disease, or you have a respiratory ailment, high blood pressure, osteoporosis, diabetes, or several risk factors for heart disease. ♥

Prime movers: Knees and hips

Mobility relies on the body's two largest joints, the hips and knees. We ask a lot of both these joints: they must bear our full weight and coordinate movement over a lifetime of standing, walking, running, dancing, and sports. Not surprisingly, hip and knee pain are common complaints, and nearly everyone who lives into old age can expect some pain or loss of function in these joints.

For people with severe pain, joint replacements and other medical advances have dramatically improved mobility. Advances in our understanding of how to care for the joints—through better preventive exercise and rehabilitation—have also helped many people regain mobility they had lost or recover from surgery more quickly. Taking care of your hips and knees and managing pain so that it doesn't slow you down will help you avoid losing mobility as you age.

How knees and hips work

Both hips and knees are feats of engineering. The knee joint is where three bones come together: the femur (thighbone), tibia (shin bone), and patella (kneecap). The simplest way to think about the knee is as a hinge that opens and closes in one plane, like the lid on a box. But in fact, the joint is more complicated than a simple hinge and allows more movement; every time you flex or extend the knee, there is a small amount of rotation, sliding, and rolling of the bones to keep them properly aligned. Muscles around the knee keep this complex movement stable.

The hip, too, is a complex joint that involves bones, muscles, and other tissues extending beyond the hip bone to the upper thigh, groin, and buttocks. The hip is a ball-and-socket joint that has a wide range of motion, so it's capable of more types of movement than the knee. When you need to, you can swing your legs out to the side, rotate them out to sit cross-legged, or circle them around in the air. Every step you take starts at the hip. But all of this mobility, combined with the need to support your body weight, makes the hip susceptible to injury, pain, and loss of mobility if any of its components isn't working correctly.

General knee and hip care

Good self-care of your joints is key to staying mobile and independent. Here are some rules of thumb to follow when you have an injury, osteoarthritis, or any health condition that affects the joints, particularly the knees, but also the hips to some extent. The same rules also apply to ankles.

RICE for acute injuries. RICE—which stands for rest, ice, compression, and elevation—is a first-aid strategy for most musculoskeletal injuries, including those involving the knees and hips. For knees, it is sometimes the only treatment you need.

- **Rest** doesn't necessarily mean lying in bed or on the couch—in fact, inactivity can make injuries worse by causing stiffness around the joints and weakening the muscles. Instead, rest means avoiding the type of activity that directly led to the injury, and trying low-impact activities that keep pressure off the joint.
- **Ice** can reduce swelling by shrinking injured blood vessels, and it also eases pain. Use a homemade or store-bought ice pack, and apply it to the injured area for 20 minutes at a time, with 20-minute pauses in between. (Note: If you use ice from your own freezer, don't apply it directly to skin, but rather make sure a layer of cloth or other material is between the ice and your skin in order to protect you from frostbite.) Devices are also available that apply continuous cold to joints using circulating cold water, but these should still be used with 20-minute breaks between cooling sessions. Ice helps knee injuries of all types. For hip injuries, cold can't penetrate deep into the hip joint itself,

but it is still effective for hip pain stemming from problems closer to the surface.

- **Compression** can promote recovery and reduce swelling after a knee injury. Wearing a stretchy neoprene support or wrapping an elastic bandage around an injured knee provides compression, but take care that the wrap isn't so tight that the skin below the joint becomes cool or blue.

- **Elevating** an injured leg on a pillow or stool can also reduce swelling by preventing blood from pooling at the injured site.

Heat therapy for long-term pain and stiffness. Icing is the best therapy in the first day or two after an injury to reduce swelling; after that, applying heat can also help ease pain. Heat reduces discomfort by relieving stiffness and promoting flexibility in the muscles. Some people like to use heat in the morning and before exercising or stretching, and ice after a workout or at the end of the day. You can use a store-bought heating pad, or heat a damp towel in the microwave at 20-second increments until it reaches the desired temperature. Make sure the heat you're applying feels warm, not hot, to avoid burning the skin. A warm bath (hydrotherapy) is a mainstay of physical therapy for joints and muscles. You don't need a professional whirlpool bath to get the benefits; soaking in a hot bath or hot tub or even taking a hot shower can work as well.

Physical therapy and exercise for injuries. Exercise has the potential to worsen joint pain and injuries, but it's also an important part of recovering from an injury or managing a health condition like osteoarthritis. Often the first treatments for joint pain will be an over-the-counter pain medication combined with physical therapy or a set of specific exercises.

A physical therapist often works with an orthopedist to help you carry out a program of movements to treat your specific condition. Physical therapy typically involves one or more sessions of supervised exercises combined with exercises that you do regularly at home. The primary goal is often to increase the range of motion in a joint, using stretches and movements that gently take a joint to the edge of its range. Another goal is to strengthen specific muscles around a joint, which can correct some joint-related problems or provide better support to a joint that's in pain. Bal-ance exercises can also help you keep joints stable and avoid injuries.

Assistive devices. A cane can often help by taking pressure off a painful hip or knee. Hold it in the opposite hand from the source of the pain. Whatever weight you place on the cane is weight taken off your hip or knee (see "Choosing a cane or walker," page 12).

How osteoarthritis can slow you down

One of the most common causes of impaired mobility is osteoarthritis of the joints, which affects 27 million Americans. It causes a breakdown of the cartilage that wraps over the ends of bones, called articular cartilage, and sometimes can affect surrounding tissues as well (see Figure 1, below). With less protective cushioning between the bones, the normally frictionless motion of the joint becomes difficult. The result is pain, swelling, stiffness, and less ability to move. If the cartilage breaks down enough over time, the bones begin to rub together, which can permanently damage the joint.

Figure 1: Joint changes in osteoarthritis

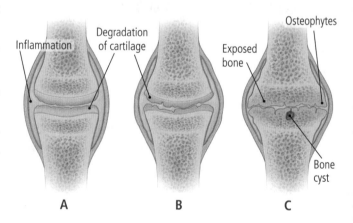

A. The first signs of osteoarthritis are microscopic pits and fissures on the cartilage surface, which are sometimes accompanied by inflammation.

B. The contours of the joint change, and the cartilage thins.

C. The bone surface thickens, and osteophytes (abnormal bony growths) develop over time. The joint may widen as the body lays down extra bone, giving it a swollen appearance, while continued thinning of cartilage leaves the bone exposed. The joint space narrows until it nearly disappears.

Osteoarthritis can occur in any joint, but the knees and hips are common sites because of the weight they bear. Osteoarthritis develops over time, and there is no known cure. The best way to prevent it is to avoid excess weight gain, to strive for a healthy weight if you're overweight, and to stay active while avoiding injuries that can happen when you put too much stress on the joints or exercise improperly.

Osteoarthritis can make it difficult to accomplish activities you once managed easily. Compensating for the diseased joints can leave muscles tired, and many people find the pain gets worse throughout the day. Osteoarthritis and other health conditions that cause chronic pain often limit movement psychologically as well as physically. People may begin to associate activity and exercise with pain, and avoid opportunities to get out and move. That's why seeking treatment for osteoarthritis can help you preserve mobility. Even if there is no way to reverse the damage, there are many ways you can manage the symptoms and maximize activity with less pain. As the disease progresses, you and your doctor can discuss whether surgery and joint replacement may be good options.

The knee is the most common site of osteoarthritis—and for reasons not entirely understood, the incidence of knee osteoarthritis is on the rise. It's also striking people earlier in life. Genes play a role in its development, as does gender (women are more likely to have it than men). The increase in overweight and obesity in the United States may be one reason why the ailment is striking younger people. Another likely factor is sports-related injuries and strain from exercise. Competitive sports and other intense activities that put pressure on joints, such as long-distance running, soccer, or weight lifting, can raise the risk of developing osteoarthritis. So we see risk rising at both extremes of the activity spectrum: both a sedentary lifestyle and a one filled with extreme activities can wind up causing problems that eventually affect mobility. That's why it's important to exercise for long-term health rather than short-term feats.

Treating osteoarthritis

If you do develop arthritis, managing it well can help keep you mobile. There is currently no proven way to

> ## Staying active with joint pain
>
> It's important to keep joints moving, even if you're dealing with pain from arthritis or an overuse injury. But sometimes you'll need to keep weight off a joint and rest it more than you usually would. Don't let a painful joint prevent you from exercising; try these joint-friendly options instead:
>
> - elliptical trainer
> - stationary bike (recumbent or upright)
> - tai chi
> - swimming, water aerobics, or water walking
> - rowing machine
> - short walks throughout the day, instead of a long walk.

reverse the damage of osteoarthritis. But treatments can help protect the joint from further damage, relieve symptoms, and keep you as active as possible. Treatments for osteoarthritis range from conservative to invasive. They include the following:

Weight loss. Although it's not clear whether losing excess weight can prevent arthritis from getting worse, it can reduce symptoms by lightening the load on joints. With each step on level ground, you put one to one-and-a-half times your body weight on each knee, so a 200-pound person can put 300 pounds of pressure on each knee. Off level ground, the news is worse: each knee bears two to three times your body weight when you go up and down stairs, and four to five times your body weight when you squat to tie a shoelace or pick up an item you dropped.

Physical therapy and exercise. Sometimes you may need to rest your joints when pain flares up, but for the most part it's important to keep exercising in order to maintain your mobility (see "Staying active with joint pain," above). Physical therapists can help you practice movements that strengthen the muscles around your knee and maintain flexibility in the joint. If you have osteoarthritis of the hip, they can show you exercises to improve the hip's range of motion and promote strength and flexibility of the surrounding muscles. They can also help with strategies for accomplishing daily tasks and activities with less pain. Exercises on your own should focus on boosting strength in the knee and moving it through its full range of motion, while avoiding high-impact activities like running and jumping that make symptoms worse.

Pain relief medications. Doctors can prescribe treatments to relieve pain and inflammation, so you can accomplish daily tasks more easily. Often, pain relief focuses on using one or more over-the-counter pain relievers such as acetaminophen (Tylenol) or nonsteroidal anti-inflammatory drugs (NSAIDs) like ibuprofen (Advil) and naproxen (Aleve). It's important to work with your doctor to find a medication regimen that works for you and then to stick to it.

Wraps, braces, and orthotics. For early, mild knee arthritis with sudden flare-ups, a simple wrap made of neoprene or elastic may help relieve pain. Because the sleeve itself doesn't provide much support to the joint, any benefit is thought to come from improvements in the knee's position and movement. A physical therapist may prescribe a variation on this type of wrap that incorporates pulsed electrical stimulation, which has proved especially effective in treating knee osteoarthritis.

Various types of braces may also help. For example, if you have arthritis affecting only one part of the knee joint, a type of brace known as an unloader brace may help by taking some of the pressure off that part of the knee and redistributing the weight. Orthotic shoe inserts may also help people with knee arthritis, because flat feet and other foot problems can affect the alignment of the ankle and knee, placing additional stress on the joints.

Injections. Injecting a long-acting corticosteroid drug into the knee or hip joint can ease pain temporarily. But most doctors avoid using this treatment too often, as it can damage some joints at frequent doses. Injections of a synthetic version of hyaluronate, a natural fluid in joints, are sometimes given to people who don't experience relief from pain medications.

Surgery. For most people, surgery is a second line of defense, used only after more conservative treatments fail or if the arthritis has progressed to a point that it is interfering with your mobility or has the potential to lead to permanent damage. Joint replacement (at right) may be the most effective approach, but there are other surgical options.

- **Arthroscopic surgery,** which is done with tiny instruments through small incisions, may be used in a joint to remove torn cartilage, debris, and loose material. This approach has been used to treat knee arthritis, but research suggests it's of limited benefit. If you have a torn meniscus as well as osteoarthritis, arthroscopic surgery to trim the meniscus may help.
- **Realignment (osteotomy)** of the knee is a procedure in which a surgeon reshapes the tibia and femur to improve the knee's alignment. It is often recommended for people with limited damage to the knee and those who are young, still highly active, or overweight.
- **Hip resurfacing** may offer an attractive alternative to traditional hip replacement, especially for younger and more active people. The surgeon reshapes the head of the thighbone and caps it with a cobalt-chromium prosthetic that fits into an artificial metal lining in the socket.
- **Cartilage replacement (chondrocyte grafting)** is a more experimental surgery that involves grafting new cartilage tissue into pockets of damaged knee cartilage. Cartilage cells can be grown in a lab from a sample from the patient's own cartilage or from a donor and then transplanted into the diseased joint. This technique appears to be most helpful for people with less severe defects in cartilage.

Joint replacement

Doctors recommend joint replacement in cases of severe osteoarthritis in which the joint shows significant deterioration. Because severe disease in the knee or hip can impede mobility, this surgery is most often recommended for those particular joints.

With knee replacement, the surgeon makes small wafer-thin cuts on the ends of the thighbone and shin bone where the two bones meet and caps them with metal implants, then uses plastic components to form the joint between them. A thick piece of plastic mounted onto the shin implant serves the same purpose as natural cartilage, allowing for smooth flowing movement. The back of the kneecap is fitted with a small plastic disc (see Figure 2, page 9).

With hip replacement, the surgeon removes the head of the thighbone and replaces it with an artificial ball (see Figure 3, below right). The ball fits into an artificial cup placed in the hip. The components are a combination of hard polished metal (generally titanium-based or cobalt/chromium-based alloy), hard ceramic, or tough, slick plastic called polyethylene.

A new knee or hip won't necessarily give you more mobility, but it can take away the pain that holds you back. Replacing a diseased joint with an artificial one brings many people relief from pain and a renewed ability to engage in daily activities, after they have recovered from the procedure. However, there are also downsides to consider, including the pain of the surgery, the long recovery, and the possibility of complications (see "Possible complications of joint replacement," page 10). After 10 to 15 years, artificial knees can also wear out and need a second surgery to replace them.

Knee and hip replacements are common: about 327,000 total hip replacements and 676,000 total knee replacements are performed in the United States each year, and those numbers are on the rise. The decision about whether and when to replace a joint is not a simple one, and replacement is recommended only after more conservative options have been tried. People are good candidates for joint replacement in these circumstances:

- They have pain that interferes with daily tasks and simple movements like walking and sitting.
- X-rays of the joint show significant damage and cartilage loss.
- Other treatments have failed or cause unpleasant side effects.

Keep in mind that a joint replacement is an elective procedure. Take as much time as you need to talk with your doctor and surgeon about your options and to understand what's best for you. A variety of artificial joints are on the market, made from different materials and with different features. The joint replacement may be full or partial (using a smaller implant that leaves part of the joint intact). The procedure may be

Figure 2: Total knee replacement

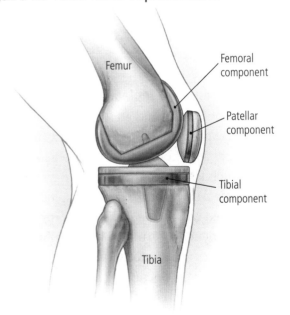

The surgeon first cuts away thin slices of bone with damaged cartilage from the end of the femur and the top of the tibia, making sure that the bones are cut to precisely fit the shape of the replacement pieces. The artificial joint is attached to the bones with cement or screws. A small plastic piece goes on the back of the kneecap (patella) to ride smoothly over the other parts of the artificial joint when you bend your knee.

Figure 3: Hip replacement surgery

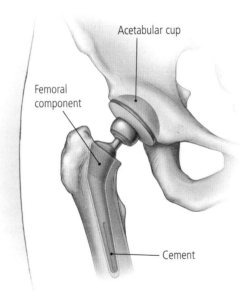

When rough and damaged cartilage prevents the bones of the hip from moving smoothly, an orthopedic surgeon can install an artificial joint with two parts. The head of the femur (thighbone) is replaced with an artificial ball with a long stem (the femoral component) that fits down inside the femur. An artificial cup, called the acetabular cup, fits inside the hip socket. The two pieces fit smoothly together to restore comfortable ball-in-socket movement.

Possible complications of joint replacement

The success rate for knee and hip replacement is very high. However, complications can occur that shorten the life of an implant, and you may need to take certain precautions.

Infection. Your implant can become infected soon after surgery or even years later. When it occurs later, it is almost always because infection elsewhere in the body has spread to the area. Seek immediate treatment if you have symptoms of an infection, particularly of the urinary tract, and inform all your doctors that you have a joint replacement.

Leg-length discrepancy. A difference in leg length occurs only rarely after knee replacement but occurs frequently, at least temporarily, after hip replacement. Before surgery, one leg is often shorter than the other—or feels shorter because the joint has deteriorated. Your orthopedic surgeon chooses an implant and plans surgery so that your legs will be equal in length after healing. After hip replacement, muscle weakness or spasm and swelling around the hip may temporarily cause an abnormal tilt to your pelvis and make you feel as though your legs are unequal in length. Stretching and strengthening exercises help restore your pelvis to its proper position. It may be several months before you can tell if the discrepancy is real and needs to be addressed with the use of a lift in one shoe. When the discrepancy is accompanied by pain, surgery can correct both problems.

Dislocation. In the weeks after a hip replacement, you'll need to take great care to keep from dislocating the implant before the surrounding tissues have healed enough to hold it in place. Even afterward, there is a chance of a painful dislocation—five out of every 100 implants dislocate after total hip replacement surgery. If your hip dislocates, your doctor gives you a sedative while he or she manipulates the implant ball back into the socket. A hip that dislocates more than once usually requires surgery to make the joint more stable.

Loosening. A replacement joint can loosen because the cement never secured it properly or eventually wore out, or because the surrounding bone did not grow into the implant well enough to create a tight attachment. This may require a second surgery.

Bone loss. As a joint implant suffers wear and tear, loose particles can drift into the joint. As your immune system attacks these foreign particles, it can also attack surrounding bone, weakening it in a process called osteolysis. This, in turn, may loosen the bone's connection to the implant. Osteolysis is a major factor leading to the need for more surgery after hip and knee replacement.

---

an open surgery or a minimally invasive procedure. The surgery itself generally takes one or two hours and requires general anesthesia. The total hospital stay is usually around two to four days but varies depending on your health status and the type of procedure.

If you need to have both hips (or both knees) replaced, this can be done in two separate surgeries several months apart, but it is also possible to have both joints replaced at the same time. The benefits of simultaneous replacement are a single anesthesia, shorter total hospitalization, and one rehabilitation that allows you to resume normal activities sooner. However, having two joints replaced at the same time increases the risk of some complications; for example, there is a slightly elevated risk of blood clots.

One of the best things you can do for a successful joint replacement is to make your joint as strong and healthy as possible beforehand. Studies have found that "prehabilitation"—exercise and strength training performed before a procedure like joint replacement surgery—can help prevent pain and boost the rate of recovery after the fact. Many clinical centers now offer "prehab" programs.

Recovering from joint replacement

A great deal of research has gone into improving strategies for recovery from joint replacement surgery and has led to greater efforts to make sure people regain mobility much faster than back in the days when they would rest for days or weeks in the hospital.

"Enhanced recovery" or "fast-track" programs for joint replacement surgeries usually combine patient education before the procedure, better use of pain medications after the operation (for example, a reduction in opioids, which cause nausea and grogginess), the use of blood thinners for an average of three weeks after the surgery in order to prevent blood clots, and starting daily tasks and exercises as soon as possible. People tend to do better when they are well prepared and know what to expect from the procedure, and when their clinicians help them start moving again immediately after surgery.

Rehabilitation begins the first day post-surgery. Often this will involve moving your leg around the joint with help from a physical therapist or a continuous passive motion (CPM) machine, which is programmed to bend and straighten the leg by ever-increasing degrees. The clinical staff will help you get out of bed and move around. Before you go home, you'll be asked to show that you can get in and out of bed without help; walk with a walker, cane, or crutches; and manage obstacles like steps that you may face at home. Directly after the procedure, you'll need assistance at home with daily tasks like shopping, cooking, and bathing.

Putting effort into your recovery is key for long-term mobility with an artificial joint. See a physical therapist regularly after the procedure; over the next weeks and months, the more you engage in exercise and physical therapy, the more successful your recovery will be. In addition to targeted exercises, you should gradually increase the distance you walk or the duration you are active so that you continue to challenge yourself. Just be careful to avoid activities like climbing stairs until you have enough strength and balance to manage them without injury (see "Dos and don'ts after joint replacement surgery," at right). By the first week or two, you should be walking with a cane (see "Choosing a cane or walker," page 12). After a few weeks, you should no longer need the cane. By three to six months you should be functioning normally.

Osteoporosis and hip fractures

Mobility relies on bones that are strong enough to handle the physical demands of life, but osteoporosis can undermine this goal. It is a progressive and often insidious condition that can gradually weaken bones without causing noticeable symptoms—until you break a bone. Fractures are extremely common; half of all women and one-quarter of all men over age 50 will have an osteoporosis-related fracture in their lifetimes. The most common places to break a bone as a result of osteoporosis are the hip, spine, and wrist.

Particularly devastating are hip fractures, which account for about one in seven fractures resulting

> ### Dos and don'ts after joint replacement surgery
> These tips can help ensure that your return to mobility goes smoothly.
>
> ✔ **Don't soak your wound.** Upon returning from the hospital, keep your wound dry until it has thoroughly sealed and dried.
>
> ✔ **Don't take risks that could cause you to fall.** Be especially careful on stairs. Use a cane, crutches, or a walker until your balance and strength have improved.
>
> ✔ **Do eat right.** Eating a healthy diet, including lots of fruits, vegetables, and whole grains, is important to promote proper tissue healing and restore muscle strength.
>
> ✔ **Do learn the signs of blood clots.** Joint replacement surgery carries a small risk of potentially dangerous blood clots, and doctors routinely prescribe anti-clotting drugs to prevent them from forming after surgery. Warning signs of a leg clot include increasing pain, tenderness, redness, or swelling in your knee and leg. Signs a clot has traveled to your lung include shortness of breath and chest pain that comes on suddenly with coughing. Call your doctor if you develop any of these signs.
>
> ✔ **Do look for signs of infection.** These include persistent fever, shaking, chills, increasing redness or swelling of the knee, drainage from the surgical site, and increasing pain with both activity and rest.
>
> ✔ **Do exercise wisely.** Performing the exercises your physical therapist recommends is crucial to restoring movement in your new joint and strengthening the surrounding muscles.

from osteoporosis. The majority of people who break a hip never fully regain their independence; about half need some kind of assistance walking, and one in four requires long-term care in a nursing home. The fracture itself is only part of the problem. Many people who experience hip fractures are elderly, and many have other medical conditions that hamper their recovery. Medical complications from the fracture or the surgery to repair it can further erode health, putting people on a downward trajectory.

How does osteoporosis sneak up on us? Bones may seem inert, but like most other tissues in the body, they contain living cells and undergo continuous changes, in a process called remodeling. For example, when blood levels of calcium fall too low, cells called osteoclasts break down bone to release calcium for other uses through the body. Cells called osteoblasts then rebuild the bone's structure, so calcium and other minerals can accumulate again. Bones also remodel to become denser with weight-bearing exercise.

Early in life, bone accumulation exceeds bone loss because our bodies are growing. But in later life, we begin to lose bone mass, as bone demolition outpaces rebuilding. Eventually the bones become more porous, weaker, and subject to fractures. Aging is the major risk factor for osteoporosis. In women, menopause leads to rapid bone loss, as estrogen levels fall.

In addition, with advancing age, the body tends to absorb less calcium from food and store it less efficiently elsewhere in the body, so it draws more on the calcium "bank account" that's stored in bones. Moreover, many people consume less calcium as they age, which only makes this deficit worse. Aging bodies also produce less vitamin D, which is important for helping the body absorb calcium from food and for creating new bone tissue. And many older people also exercise less, so bones do not receive the same signals to bulk up.

Finally, in addition to these normal changes, medical conditions such as cancer, liver disease, hyperparathyroidism (an overactive parathyroid gland),

Choosing a cane or walker

Your goal may be to avoid assistive devices as long as possible, but in some cases a cane or walker can help you maintain your mobility and avoid further disability—for example, if you're recovering from an injury or surgery, struggling with arthritis, or managing a balance impairment. If your doctor recommends a cane or walker, don't let your stubbornness or sense of pride keep you from using it; about 30% to 50% of people stop using devices that are prescribed to them. But these simple tools have been shown to improve stability, prevent falls and injuries, and take the load off areas of pain.

Canes generally come in standard, offset, and multiple-legged versions:

Standard canes. These are the simplest canes, and are usually lightweight and inexpensive. They usually have a curved or T-shaped handle (many people find a T-shaped handle more comfortable). A standard cane is good for helping with balance but not for bearing a lot of weight.

Offset canes. The upper shaft of an offset cane bends outward, and the handle grip is usually flat—it is a better choice for people who need the cane to bear more weight or who have a weak grip.

Multiple-legged canes. Multiple legs offer considerable support and allow the cane to stand on its own when not in use. One drawback to using such a cane is that for maximum support, you must plant all the legs solidly on the ground, which can slow down your walking speed.

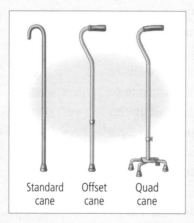

Standard cane   Offset cane   Quad cane

To use a cane, hold it in the hand opposite the side that needs support, about four inches to the side of your stronger leg. Always consult with a knowledgeable physical therapist or other clinician to select a cane and choose the proper height. Make sure you know how to use it properly. The cane should be part of a larger plan for your mobility, which may include muscle-strengthening exercises, a treatment plan for a condition, and regular walks and physical activity. Canes are available at medical supply stores and pharmacies, through specialty catalogs, and on the Internet. Insurance usually covers the cost of a basic cane if you have a written prescription from your doctor.

Walkers come in three configurations: four rubber-tip legs; two wheels and two nonwheel legs; or four wheels. Walkers with four wheels are easier to move forward quickly, but make it more difficult to put weight on the walker. They usually have bars that are parallel to the ground with hard plastic or soft foam grips. The top of the walker should line up with the crease of your wrist when your arms are down at your sides.

It takes some getting used to walking, sitting down, standing up, and going up and down steps safely with a walker. Make sure you get some training from your doctor or physical therapist. All four tips or wheels should be on the ground before you take a step or put weight on it to rise from a chair. Keep some distance between yourself and the walker as you move, to avoid tripping on it, and keep your torso upright to maintain good posture. You may also need to rearrange rugs or furniture at home to avoid catching the walker on objects.

and anorexia can lead to osteoporosis. Some medications—including corticosteroids, proton-pump inhibitors, aromatase inhibitors for breast cancer, and androgen inhibitors for prostate cancer—can also promote bone loss or weakness. Your lifestyle and habits influence bone health, too: if you don't consume enough calcium and vitamin D, are a smoker, drink too much alcohol, or don't get enough physical activity, you are at higher risk of developing osteoporosis. Among women, osteoporosis is more common in Caucasian and Asian women than in those of other ethnic backgrounds, and in women who are thin and small-boned or very low in body fat.

Preventing osteoporosis

While it's true that all people lose bone as they age, osteoporosis is not inevitable.

Exercise. The best way to protect bone health is with regular exercise. When you put force on your bones, it prompts your body to build new bone. Types of exercise in which you carry your own weight, like walking, hiking, or aerobics, are good for keeping the bones in your legs and hips strong. But there are a couple of rules of thumb to remember if you're aiming for maximum effect on bone *and* you are able to work out vigorously.

- Generally, higher-impact activities have a more pronounced effect on bone than lower-impact exercises; sports such as tennis, volleyball, or running build bone faster than walking or low-impact aerobics.
- Velocity is also a factor; jogging or fast-paced aerobics will do more to strengthen bone than more leisurely movement.
- Only those bones that bear the load of the exercise will benefit. For example, walking or running protects only the bones in your lower body.

If you are unable to work out vigorously, try low-impact exercises, such as tai chi, swimming, or the strengthening exercises on page 25.

Diet. Make sure your diet has all the nutrients it needs to keep building bone.

- **Calcium** is the main ingredient of bone. Dairy foods provide the most concentrated sources, but you can also find calcium in such foods as sockeye salmon, sardines, fortified orange juice, spinach, dried beans, nuts, and tofu made with calcium sulfate.
- **Vitamin D** helps the body absorb calcium. The body makes its own vitamin D when sunlight hits skin. Unfortunately, vitamin D is naturally found in only a few foods, such as salmon, tuna, mackerel, and fish liver oils. It's also added to most milk in the United States and some other products (such as breakfast cereals, orange juice, and yogurt).
- **Vitamin K** helps produce a protein involved in making bone. Studies have found that people who take in higher levels of vitamin K are less likely to break hips. Vitamin K is found in broccoli, Brussels sprouts, leafy greens, and cabbage.

Whether you get these nutrients from foods or from supplements will depend somewhat on your diet and your health risks (see "Do you need supplements?" on page 41).

Bone-building medications. Medications can also play a key role in preventing and treating osteoporosis. These drugs include

- bisphosphonates, such as alendronate (Fosamax), ibandronate (Boniva), risedronate (Actonel), and zoledronic acid (Reclast)
- estrogen (Premarin, Estrace, others)
- the selective estrogen receptor modulator raloxifene (Evista)
- the monoclonal antibody denosumab (Prolia). ◗

A good foundation: Feet and ankles

Your feet are literally the foundation of your mobility. They have a complex structure with over 50 bones and even more joints, all designed to manage pressure, weight, and force, while being extremely flexible. Each foot consists of three basic parts: the forefoot (the toes and ball of your foot), the midfoot (the arch), and the hindfoot (the heel).

Foot pain can arise at any age, but many of the problems that emerge in feet are products of wear and tear, so they become more frequent with age. Chronic foot pain is a common complaint of seniors and one of the reasons many people limit their movement with age. Foot problems can also lead to falls, and thus to broken bones, which can be disastrous for mobility.

Common foot problems

Feet are complex structures that are subject to a host of problems (see Figure 4, at right), but these are the ones that most frequently limit mobility.

Achilles' tendinitis and Achilles' tendinosis. Heel pain may occur when the Achilles' tendon, which runs up the back of the heel, suffers damage, inflammation, or degeneration. With Achilles' tendinitis, the tendon becomes inflamed. A separate yet related problem, Achilles' tendinosis, occurs when the tendon actually degrades—much like a rope fraying. Because the symptoms and treatment of these two problems are virtually the same, you may not know whether you have Achilles' tendinitis or tendinosis unless you ask your doctor. Many patients have both disorders. But it's good to know, because if you develop Achilles' tendinosis, it's vital that you take steps to protect your tendon from further structural damage.

The Achilles' tendon has a tendency to become inflamed and degraded, often because of overexertion from running or other high-impact activities, weight gain, or wearing ill-fitting shoes.

The condition is usually treated with a combination of approaches, including the RICE first-aid regimen (see "RICE for acute injuries," page 5), pain relievers, and light stretching exercises. Special night splints and footwear inserts can also provide relief.

Bunions and bunionettes. A bunion often looks like a growth on the side of the foot at the base of the big toe. But it is actually a misalignment of the bones, causing the big toe to turn inward, toward (or sometimes under) the other toes. Bunions are the most common toe problem and are more common in women than in men. A bunionette is a similar condition that affects the base of the smallest toe.

Because the most frequent cause of bunions and bunionettes is wearing shoes with cramped toe boxes,

Figure 4: Sites where structural problems occur

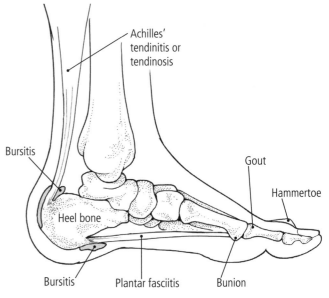

© Harriet Greenfield

The foot is a complex structure and can experience a variety of structural problems or injuries. Among the more common of these are Achilles' tendinitis, Achilles' tendinosis, bursitis, plantar fasciitis, bunions and bunionettes, hammertoes, and more.

wearing roomier shoes is the best step to take to prevent them from forming (see "Shoes: What to wear?" at right). Roomy shoes, shoe inserts, and special pads can also help relieve pain, as can hot and cold compresses. In severe cases, surgery may be required (see Figure 5, page 16), but it is a major procedure that requires you to stay off your feet and avoid driving for several weeks.

Hammertoes. Another cause of toe pain is a hammertoe, a deformity that develops when tendons and ligaments in a toe contract, causing the toe to bend over and curl up—resembling a hammer. The top of your toe may then rub against your shoe, causing irritation, corns, calluses, or even bursitis. The problem usually develops in the second toe, often because a bunion has formed in the big toe, forcing it inward and displacing the second toe. Shoes with narrow toe boxes, which compress the toes, increase the risk for a hammertoe. Usually hammertoes are flexible at first; that is, if you apply pressure to the toe, it will flatten back down. But over time, a hammertoe can become rigid and may become more painful and inflamed.

You can relieve hammertoe pain by applying ice or cold compresses or by soaking your foot in warm water. For severe cases, surgery may be necessary.

Bursitis. A bursa is a fluid-filled sac that cushions a tendon near a bone. If a bursa becomes inflamed, the painful condition is known as bursitis.

To prevent posterior heel bursitis, make sure that your shoes fit correctly and provide plenty of cushioning. The condition is generally treated like Achilles' tendinitis, with the RICE regimen (see "RICE for acute injuries," page 5) and nonprescription pain relievers. It can take between six and 12 months to heal.

Osteoarthritis of the feet. If osteoarthritis develops in the toes or other foot bones, it can cause pain and stiffness in the feet and can affect your normal gait, causing you to favor one side or limp. Obesity and previous foot injuries are major risk factors for foot osteoarthritis.

The condition can be alleviated with gentle stretching exercises like the ones in this section (see "Stretching the ankles and feet," page 18). You can also reduce pain and any inflammation with hot and cold packs, NSAIDs, or a COX-2 inhibitor such as

Shoes: What to wear?

These days, comfort shoes have become much better looking, and even stylish dress shoes can be found that are easier on feet.

Look for shoes that have a wide toe box that doesn't squeeze your toes together. Women are especially prone to buying shoes that are too small, and the vast majority of foot problems in women come from wearing tight shoes. One helpful tip is to shop for shoes in the afternoon when your feet have expanded slightly, to keep you from choosing too-tight shoes. And wear the socks or stockings that you would expect to wear with the shoes. Don't be shy about asking to get your foot measured by a salesperson—most people's feet get slightly larger and wider as they age, so your size may need adjustment over time.

Also make sure the shoe offers plenty of support. Many shoes today are being designed with composite soles to offer extra shock absorption. When looking for athletic shoes, always choose shoes that are designed for the activity you'll be doing and that provide plenty of cushioning and support. Make sure they are roomy enough so that your toes don't hit the front of the shoe as you move.

For daily use, women should opt for shoes with a low heel—no higher than three-quarters of an inch. The higher the heel, the worse it will be for your feet, even if the heels are wide.

For the names of shoe manufacturers that have earned the American Podiatric Medical Association's Seal of Acceptance, visit www.apma.org.

celecoxib (Celebrex). Your doctor may also recommend shoe inserts to adjust your walking gait in a way that will take pressure off aching joints. If these strategies don't alleviate your arthritis pain, surgery to repair or replace damaged joints may be necessary. To help protect your feet from injury—which can lead to osteoarthritis—wear well-fitting, well-built shoes with cushioned soles (see "Shoes: What to wear?" above).

Calluses and corns. Calluses are broad areas of thick skin that usually form on the bottom of the feet as a protective response against the wear and tear of walking, a structural abnormality in the feet, or shoes that rub. Corns are smaller, hard growths and usually develop on the top or sides of toes, or softer ones between toes. They often arise from wearing tight shoes. Some hardening of the skin on feet is normal, but sometimes it can lead to pain or trouble walking.

Better-fitting shoes will reduce the irritation that caused the problem in the first place, and over time, the corns or calluses will shrink on their own. But don't expect overnight results; the process will take weeks or even months.

If you can't wait that long, you can treat the problem on your own in most cases (the exceptions being if you have diabetes, peripheral neuropathy, or some other circulatory problem; in those cases, never try to treat a corn or callus yourself, or you may develop an infection). Otherwise, you can remove dead skin by soaking feet in warm water and gently rubbing the area with a pumice stone or foot file. Afterward, moisturize the area with skin lotion. The key word is gentle; don't overdo it, or you could hurt your skin. For larger corns and calluses, consult a foot care specialist, who will shave away some of the thickened skin.

Figure 5: Surgical correction of a bunion

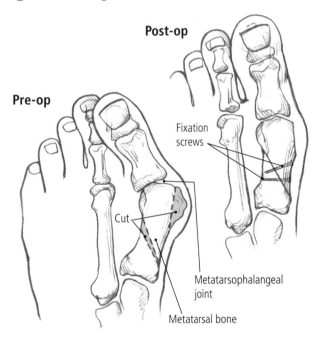

© Harriet Greenfield

The procedure illustrated above, known as a proximal osteotomy, is used to correct a severe bunion. First, the surgeon cuts away a portion of the bunion at the head of the metatarsal bone. Next, he or she removes a pie-shaped segment from the lower portion of the same bone, allowing for realignment of the metatarsophalangeal joint. Two pins or screws fasten the bone segments.

Plantar fasciitis. The plantar fascia is a strong band of tissue on the underside of the foot that connects the ball of your foot to the heel. It's highly susceptible to becoming irritated and inflamed, and this condition (plantar fasciitis) is a common cause of heel pain.

Plantar fasciitis may get better on its own, but you may be able to speed healing. When pain comes on, lightly stretch the foot and ice it. Taking NSAIDs can help control pain and inflammation. Physical therapy for plantar fasciitis, which includes a program of exercises to stretch the heel and bottom of the foot, can also help. Physical therapists also sometimes pair exercises with extracorporeal shock wave therapy, which uses high-energy sound waves to reduce pain.

Gout. Gout is a form of arthritis that occurs when uric acid, a normal byproduct of digestion, accumulates in the joints and forms crystals. The big toe is a common site for symptoms, which include stabbing pain, redness, and swelling. Gout is more common than women than in men, but in women the risk increases after age 50, because uric acid levels increase after menopause. Certain foods with high levels of substances called purines (including sardines, lentils, mussels, scallops, anchovies, and organ meats) can increase uric acid levels.

Gout is usually treated with pain relievers, steroid injections, prescription medications, and changes in the diet.

Keeping feet healthy

Feet are easy to neglect. But taking a few simple steps to care for your feet should be part of your overall strategy for maintaining mobility.

Maintain a healthy weight. Being overweight affects your feet by putting greater force on them with each step. It can increase your risk of having a condition like arthritis in the feet, and it can worsen pain from other foot problems. Being overweight can also harm foot health by putting you at higher risk for diabetes or poor blood circulation, which can lead to foot pain and loss of sensation in the feet.

Wear good shoes. Many of the common foot problems described here have tight, poorly fitting shoes as the culprit. Foot specialists shake their heads at some of the shoes people wear, particularly women. It's estimated that eight in 10 women wear shoes that are painful, and those wearing ill-fitting shoes are nine times as likely to develop a foot problem. Shoe fashions come and go, but a lifetime of wearing comfortable shoes is one of the best preventive measures you can take to ensure your mobility (see "Shoes: What to wear?" on page 15). Wearing tight shoes or high heels now and then for a night out won't cause lasting damage. But when you know you'll be on your feet most of the day, choose supportive, comfortable shoes. Invest in well-fitting athletic shoes for running, aerobics, and other high-impact activities.

Moisturize your feet. The skin of the feet tends to get thinner and drier with age; calloused feet can crack and bleed, causing pain. To keep the skin soft, rub a thick moisturizing lotion into your feet after showers or baths as needed (avoid the spaces in between the toes, where moisture can lead to bacterial overgrowth).

Practice good foot hygiene. As people age, it can become harder and harder to reach the feet. Wash and dry your feet thoroughly when you shower or bathe. Cut toenails straight across to avoid ingrown nails (see "Helpful hint," above). Use a pumice stone or foot file to gently remove calluses. If you wear nail polish, let the toenails "breathe" for a couple of days after you remove it and before adding more, to keep nails healthy.

Stretch your feet. People don't usually think about stretching the tops and bottoms of their feet, but stretches can help you treat—and prevent—foot pain. Stretches for the Achilles' tendon are also important (see "Stretching the ankles and feet," page 18).

Active ankles

Your ankles make important contributions to movement. The ankle is a joint made of three bones: the tibia (shin bone), the fibula (a thin bone that runs parallel to the tibia on the inside of the leg), and the talus (the central ankle bone that sits at the top of the foot). The bony bumps you feel on the outside and inside of the ankle are part of the tibia and fibula. The talus sits between these two bumps and works like a hinge to allow you to point and flex your foot. The ankle also has joints to permit sideways movement.

Ankle sprains, which involve the stretching or tearing of ligaments in the ankle joint, are extremely common. Whenever you land improperly on your feet and cause your ankle to roll to one side or to twist, it can cause a sprain that is mild to severe. The setback is usually temporary, but frequent sprains can cause long-term problems.

Ankle sprains are more common in people who have loose ligaments or weak ankle muscles. Both make the ankle more likely to twist or bend accidentally. A poor sense of balance—including any problems in sensing touch or the position of your foot in space—can contribute to sprains and falls. Sprains should be treated with the RICE method (see "RICE for acute injuries," page 5). Exercises to strengthen the ankles and preserve balance can help you prevent sprains (see "Balance exercises," page 30).

Some people develop osteoarthritis of the ankle, particularly ballet dancers who have subjected the ankles to years of stress, or people with foot conditions that put an extra burden on ankles. Special ankle braces, boots, or shoe inserts can ease the pain of ankle arthritis. Unlike hips and knees, ankles cannot be surgically replaced. Severe cases of ankle arthritis are sometimes treated with surgery that fuses two bones together.

Exercises to improve ankle strength and flexibility are an important addition to the exercises for hips and knees, to maintain your mobility or to improve ankle strength. Exercising your ankles also builds your sensory awareness of these essential joints, making you less likely to fall or twist an ankle (see "Stretching the ankles and feet," page 18). ♥

Stretching the ankles and feet

Stretching the feet and ankles is often a component of physical therapy for foot pain; it's also a good practice to maintain mobility in your feet and ankles. These simple stretching exercises can be done as a short addition to your daily routine.

Limber up

To limber up your foot before attempting other exercises, try this:

1. Sit in a chair with your feet flat on the floor.

2. Lift your left leg so your foot is off the floor and use your big toe to make circles in the air, moving in a clockwise direction, for 15 to 20 rotations.

3. Reverse direction and make another 15 to 20 circles, this time in a counter-clockwise direction.

4. Repeat with your right foot.

Bottom of foot

To stretch the muscles on the bottom of your feet:

1. Stand with feet together.

2. Step back with your left leg so your heel is raised and your toes press against the ground. You should feel the muscles on the bottom of your feet pull gently.

3. Hold for 20 to 30 seconds.

4. Repeat with your right foot.

Top of foot

To stretch the muscles on top of your feet:

1. Stand on a phone book, which should be placed on a nonslippery floor (like a carpet), with the balls of your feet near the edge so your toes extend into free space.

2. Curl your toes slowly downward, as if you were trying to open the book. Hold for 20 to 30 seconds (or however long you can; you may need to build up to this). You should feel a pull on the top of your feet and toes.

3. Step off the book. Now, working with one foot at a time, raise your heel and curl your toes under, pressing the tops of your toes against the floor. You should feel the muscles on the top of your feet and the front of your ankle gently stretch.

4. Hold for 20 to 30 seconds.

5. Repeat with the other foot.

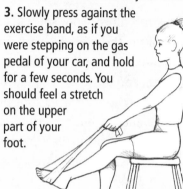

Achilles' tendon (runner's stretch)

To stretch your Achilles' tendon:

1. Stand at arm's length from a wall, pressing your hands against it and keeping your feet together.

2. Step back with your left leg, bending

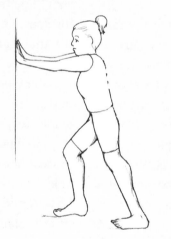

your right knee slightly and keeping the left heel on the ground. You should feel a stretch along your calf to your ankle. Hold for 20 to 30 seconds.

3. Repeat with your right leg.

Ankle strength

You can practice a simple exercise to increase ankle strength that mimics the movement of your foot when you press down on an accelerator or clutch in a car:

1. Sit in a chair with your feet flat on the floor, pointing forward.

2. Lift your left leg. Hold the ends of an exercise band and place the center of the band under the ball of your foot.

3. Slowly press against the exercise band, as if you were stepping on the gas pedal of your car, and hold for a few seconds. You should feel a stretch on the upper part of your foot.

Then release.

4. Repeat 10 to 15 times.

5. Repeat with your right leg.

Heel exercises

To stretch the back of your heel:

1. Loop an exercise band around the leg of a heavy piece of furniture, such as a table or desk.

2. Sitting directly in front of it, slip your foot into the loop so the exercise band curls around your forefoot, just below your toes.

3. Pull back with your forefoot, flexing at the ankle. Hold for several seconds, then relax. You should feel a stretch along the back of your heel.

4. Repeat 10 to 15 times.

5. Repeat with your other foot.

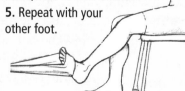

A stable support: Your back and posture

Your hips, legs, and feet make walking possible, but the health of your spine and your ability to maintain good posture are essential to moving effectively. Your spine and the muscles that support it hold your body upright and give you the stability to do all your daily activities, even one as simple as holding yourself upright in a chair.

Figure 6: Regions of the spine

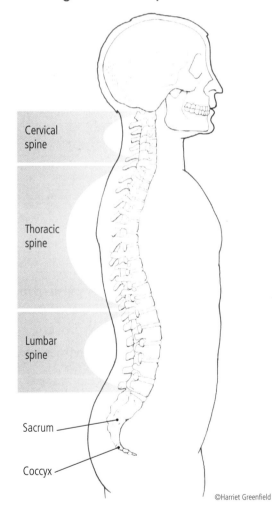

Cervical spine

Thoracic spine

Lumbar spine

Sacrum

Coccyx

©Harriet Greenfield

Your spine is divided into three regions: the cervical, the thoracic, and the lumbar. Low back pain originates in the lumbar area, which extends from the bottom of your rib cage to your sacrum (the triangular bone found between your hip bones).

Your spine is a remarkable structure that is asked to perform a difficult set of tasks over a lifetime. Although we often think of a "straight back" as good posture, the spine can be divided into three areas, each of which has a gentle curve (see Figure 6, at left). These curves make it easier for the back to support the weight of the body, but if they become too exaggerated, it can make movement much more difficult.

The spine is made of many individual bones called vertebrae. The lower they are, the larger they are. These bones provide postural support for the body. They also protect the spinal cord. This large bundle of nerves, about as thick as one of your fingers, carries messages between the brain and the body. The spinal cord starts at the base of the skull and travels down through spaces in each vertebra. Along its length, branching nerves, called nerve roots, leave the spinal cord, poke out through holes in the vertebrae, and travel to different parts of the body. Cervical nerves in the neck are responsible for movement and sensation in the arms, neck, and upper trunk. Thoracic nerves in the upper back connect to the trunk and abdomen. Lumbar and sacral nerves in the lower back connect to the bladder, bowel, sexual organs, and legs.

Like other skeletal structures, the spine is subject to age-related health problems from osteoarthritis or osteoporosis in the vertebrae. Back pain—whether from a medical condition or an injury—is something that nearly everyone experiences at some time or other. If it becomes chronic, it can keep you from being active and remaining fully engaged in your life. When something goes wrong in the spine, it can cause not only back pain but also numbness or loss of movement in the areas the nerves supply.

Sprains, strains, and chronic pain

Back pain can have several different causes. The most common cause for sudden, temporary back pain is a sprain or strain due to overuse, unaccustomed activity, excessive lifting, or an accident of some kind. This is usually relieved by over-the-counter pain medications and generally clears up in days to weeks. In addition, it can help to apply an ice pack immediately following the injury, since this can numb the area and prevent or reduce swelling caused by inflammation. Apply on and off for 20 minutes at a time. After 48 hours, though, applying heat may be more helpful, to warm and soothe aching muscles and increase blood flow. And limit bed rest during the day to a few hours.

But back pain can also be a sign of problems in the spine itself, such as a disc that bulges out from its normal position (herniates) or ruptures, putting pressure on nerves that travel out of the spinal cord to the lower body. Or the pain could be a sign of compression fractures in the vertebrae resulting from osteoporosis (see "Compression fractures," page 23). The spine is particularly vulnerable to developing osteoporosis, because the main component of vertebrae is a spongy type of bone that is more easily weakened by osteoporosis. Spinal stenosis (see page 22)—a narrowing of the spinal canal—is another common cause of back pain in people over age 50. And, like other joints in the body, the spinal joints can also develop osteoarthritis.

Back pain is one of the top reasons that people begin to lose mobility in middle age. Pain can keep people from engaging in physical activity, making it more difficult for them to maintain a healthy weight and keep up their strength, stamina, and balance as they age. So treating and managing back pain that results from injuries or health problems is crucial for staying on the path of a healthy and active life.

If you're experiencing lower back pain that is intense or lasts more than a couple of weeks, see your doctor to get a proper diagnosis; x-rays and other imaging tests can help determine if there's underlying damage to the vertebrae or discs.

Exercise, good posture, and other back-healthy habits

Whether you're experiencing a single episode of back pain or a chronic problem, it's important to stay active (unless your doctor says not to). Even in the case of temporary muscle strains, bed rest can make the problem worse by letting the muscles that support your back weaken and stiffen without use.

In fact, rehabilitative exercise can help lessen chronic low back pain for many people. There is evidence that practicing yoga can help too. But yoga classes and instructors are highly variable, and yoga can also injure the back if you overstretch or push yourself into difficult poses—so opt for a class that is gentle, and modify poses as needed to avoid injury.

Any exercise program for back pain should be customized to meet your needs and introduced gradually. One golden rule about any exercise plan is to stop if it becomes painful. Exercise is meant to help, not hurt. If you were exercising before an episode of back pain and then had to slow down or stop for a while because of the pain, don't resume exercising at

---

Figure 7: The laws of lifting

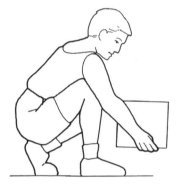

Follow these basic steps whenever you need to lift something:

1. Face the object and position yourself close to it.

2. Bend at your knees, not your waist, and squat down as far as you comfortably can.

3. Tighten your stomach and keep your buttocks tucked in.

4. Lift with your legs, not your back muscles.

5. Don't try to lift the object too high. Don't raise a heavy load any higher than your waist; keep a light load below shoulder level.

6. Keep the object close to you as you lift it.

7. If you need to turn to set something down, don't twist your upper body. Instead, turn your entire body, moving your shoulders, hips, and feet at the same time.

8. Ask for help with lifting anything that's too heavy.

What type of mattress is best for people with low back pain?

Considering that most people spend roughly a third of their lives lying in bed, choosing the right mattress is an important matter. And if you have low back pain, it can make the difference in whether you can sleep at night and function the next day. While there's not a great deal of research on this topic, a few studies offer some guidance.

In the past, doctors often recommended very firm mattresses. But one study, based on a waiting-room survey of 268 people with low back pain, found that those who slept on orthopedic (very hard) mattresses had the poorest sleep quality. There was no difference in sleep quality between those who used medium-firm and firm mattresses.

Another report, in which 313 people slept on a medium-firm or firm mattress for three months, found that those with the medium-firm mattresses reported less pain when lying in bed and less pain-related disability in general than those using firm mattresses.

Soft mattresses, on the other hand, may be problematic. While a soft mattress that conforms to your body's natural curves may help the joints align favorably, you might also sink in so deeply that your joints twist and become painful during the night. For older people, a soft mattress may also make it harder to get up and out of bed easily for late-night trips to the bathroom.

If you want to find out if a firmer mattress would feel better than the one you're currently using, try putting a plywood board under your mattress to dampen the movement from the bedsprings, or try placing your mattress on the floor.

Of course, you can also go to a mattress showroom and test a variety of models. But keep in mind that what feels comfortable for a few minutes in a store might not translate into a good night's sleep. A more reliable test, if you spend a night at a hotel or at someone else's house, is to observe how you feel after sleeping on that type of mattress.

---

the same level as before the episode. Deconditioning occurs quickly; if you try to pick up your exercise routine where you left off, you might get hurt. Start by doing less (fewer minutes or fewer repetitions) and gradually build back up to where you were before.

Weak back and abdominal muscles, resulting from deconditioning or age, cause or worsen many cases of low back pain. That's why stretching and strengthening your back and your abdominal muscles is important not only for treating low back pain, but also for helping to prevent a recurrence of the problem. Exercise strengthens and stretches the muscles that support the spine. (See "Strengthening your core," page 26, for one simple strengthening exercise.)

Practicing good posture when exercising, as well as in your daily life, not only prevents injuries but also helps you condition the muscles that keep you upright and supported in your everyday activity. It's helpful to use a mirror at first to check your posture and alignment. Good posture when standing means
- your chin parallel to the floor
- shoulders rolled back and down evenly
- arms at your sides, elbows relaxed and even
- abdominal muscles pulled in
- weight evenly placed over your hips and feet (not shifting to one side or another)

- your knees and feet pointing straight ahead.

Good posture can help not only when you're exercising, but also when you're carrying out everyday tasks, such as lifting things (see Figure 7, page 20). In addition, you can take some of the pressure of your back by following some simple steps:
- While standing to perform ordinary tasks like chopping vegetables or folding laundry, keep one foot on a small step stool.
- When sitting, keep your knees a bit higher than your hips and bend them at a 90-degree angle. Sit with your feet comfortably on the floor. If your feet don't reach the floor, put a book or small stool under them.
- Don't remain seated or standing in the same position for too long. Stretch, shift your position, or take a short walk. Make frequent stops when driving long distances.
- Sleep on your side if you can, and bend your knees toward your chest a bit. Also choose a pillow that keeps your head level with your spine; your pillow shouldn't prop your head up too high or let it droop. Choose a mattress that's firm enough to support your spine but also follows your body's contours (see "What type of mattress is best for people with low back pain?" above).

Nerve-compression syndromes

After sprains and strains, the next most common category of low back pain consists of conditions involving compressed nerves (often referred to as "pinched" nerves). Two major examples are disc problems, such as a herniated disc, and spinal stenosis, which occurs when a narrowing of the spinal column puts pressure on nerves in the spine.

Disc abnormalities

As a disc degenerates over time, its gelatinous center tends to dry out. The layers of the outer shell often start to tear, thin, and weaken, especially in the parts of the disc closest to the nerve roots. A disc with these changes tends to bulge, looking like an underinflated tire. Herniation occurs when the inner core of the disc bulges out of the outer shell. People commonly refer to this as a "slipped disc" or "ruptured disc."

This kind of pressure usually causes inflammation and back pain, often accompanied by sciatica—a sharp pain that runs along the path of the sciatic nerve, which passes through the buttock, down the leg, and into the foot.

Disc problems take longer to heal than simple sprains and strains. But 90% of people with sciatica or herniated discs will recover on their own within six months. For chronic pain, the best approach is a program combining pain-relieving medication, physical activity, and a complementary therapy such as acupuncture. If the pain still persists, your doctor may refer you to a pain clinic. These centers use a variety of approaches, including cognitive behavioral therapy, exercise programs, biofeedback, relaxation techniques, and selective nerve blocks to ease the pain or minimize its effect on your daily routine.

Spinal stenosis

The spinal cord travels through spaces in the vertebrae. If these spaces narrow for any reason, this puts pressure on the spinal cord and the spinal nerve roots. This condition is called spinal stenosis. In the lower back, spinal stenosis can affect mobility.

Nearly half of people in their 60s have some spinal stenosis in the lower back. It's the leading reason people get spinal surgery at that age. Symptoms include pain that begins in the buttocks and radiates down the legs (sciatica) and sometimes back pain. Some people feel numbness and tingling in those areas, or even just weakness and fatigue. You may feel pain or cramping when standing for long periods of time or walking, and the pain usually lessens when you're seated—particularly if you lean forward, which allows the spine to stretch out. (In contrast, many other types of lower back pain feel worse with sitting for long periods.)

The condition can be treated with surgery, but most physicians recommend trying conservative treatments first. Treatments include medications, such as NSAIDs to lessen inflammation and pain. Muscle relaxants, opioid medications, the antiseizure drug gabapentin (Neurontin), and some antidepressants like amitriptyline (Elavil) can help ease chronic pain. Always use these drugs under a doctor's supervision, as they can have potentially harmful side effects, such as dampening breathing during sleep. As with other types of joint pain, occasional injections of corticosteroids that quell inflammation can sometimes help.

Physical therapy can't heal the narrowing of the spinal column, but it can improve the overall strength and flexibility of the spine, and it may help with managing pain and numbness from the condition. If you're struggling with spinal stenosis, adopting a regular exercise schedule that includes walking and light stretching can help you preserve your mobility as you work with your doctor to treat the condition.

When conservative treatments don't work, a procedure called decompression laminectomy is an option. It involves removing a thin piece of bone called the lamina at the back part of an affected vertebra to reduce pressure on the spinal cord. Spinal fusion, which involves using a bone graft taken from the hip or pelvis to fuse two vertebrae together, is another option. A third option, called interspinous spacer implantation, uses small metal devices implanted between spinous processes—the projections of the vertebrae that form the bumps close to your skin along your spine—in order to reduce the pressure on spinal nerves. Although the procedure is minimally invasive with a quick recovery time, people who have spacer implants are more likely to need surgery again.

Compression fractures

Fractures of the spine are more common than hip fractures—and unlike hip bones, vertebrae can break without a sudden fall or injury. Instead, the constant weight bearing down on the vertebrae can compress them over time. Rather than snapping, the bones collapse. Viewed from the side, vertebrae with compression fractures often look like wedges rather than level discs. Compression fractures can cause a person to lose height as the spine shrinks or to develop a hunched posture (see "Hyperkyphosis," below).

Some spinal fractures cause little or no pain, and the only symptoms are the effects on the shape of the spine. In other cases, they can cause pain that is either sharp or dull and may radiate around the side of the body. They can also provoke spasms in muscles around the spine.

Spinal fractures can take a major toll on mobility. Over time, posture becomes distorted, and the core muscles that normally maintain an upright posture weaken. People with spinal fractures can have difficulty walking and maintaining balance and may rely on a cane or other assistive device to move around (see "Choosing a cane or walker," page 12).

The standard treatment has long been to wait it out while the fractured bone heals. This process can take six weeks on average and is very painful; often narcotic painkillers are necessary to provide relief.

In some cases, either of two procedures might be used to treat vertebral fractures: vertebroplasty and kyphoplasty. Both involve injecting surgical cement into the compressed vertebra to fill holes and crevices. But there are no large trials yet that confirm that these techniques are effective.

Hyperkyphosis

You may know someone, or have seen someone, whose back hunches over in an exaggerated way. That's a condition called "dowager's hump." In medical lingo, it's called age-related postural hyperkyphosis. The problem is more than cosmetic: it can limit mobility and raise the risk of falls and fractures.

People with this condition are more likely to have trouble getting out of a chair without using their hands (see "The 'get up and go' test," page 3), have poorer balance, walk more slowly up stairs, and have a slowed or abnormal gait. They report greater difficulties with daily tasks like housework and an overall lower quality of life. Over time, the abnormal posture can lead to further joint problems, a higher risk of fractures, and difficulty breathing properly.

Why some people begin to hunch over isn't completely clear. In some cases, a weakening or degeneration in the bones is to blame. Many people who have the condition have also experienced compression fractures in their vertebrae, in which part of the bone weakens and collapses.

But not all people whose backs begin to bend have had vertebral fractures. Weakness in the muscles and connective tissue that are important for maintaining upright posture can also cause hyperkyphosis. Age-related decreases in sensory awareness—such as the sense of balance and the body's position in space—may also lead people to gradually fail to maintain proper posture.

There's no easy treatment for hyperkyphosis. Targeted exercises designed to strengthen postural muscles and improve flexibility can help, as long as they are the right kind of exercises. Exercises that flex the spine—those with movements in which you bend forward or curl up, including abdominal curls—can put undue stress on the vertebrae and have been linked with higher rates of fractures in women with hyperkyphosis. In contrast, spine extension exercises, which involve gentle backward bending of the spine, may help counteract hyperkyphosis. Other treatments include wearing braces, wearing a special weighted vest, or applying therapeutic tape across the shoulder blades and upper back to encourage a more upright posture.

The best prevention for hyperkyphosis is to maintain good posture and strengthen muscles in the abdomen and back. Some studies suggest that types of exercise that promote flexibility in the back, such as tai chi and yoga, can help prevent the condition from developing. Since the health of your bones also contributes to the shape of your spine, taking steps to protect bone health and treat osteoporosis are also important. ◆

Masterful muscles

More than 600 muscles work together to allow you to accomplish all the movements you make every day. Yet a process called sarcopenia—a gradual decrease in muscle tissue—can rob you of muscle mass and strength. Older people who have lost muscle become increasingly frail, and previously effortless activities like lifting a trash bag, climbing stairs, vacuuming the house, or getting dressed can start to feel burdensome. Such individuals are more likely to injure themselves and are less likely to recover easily. They depend more and more on others to do tasks they once accomplished themselves.

Between the ages of 30 and 70, the average person loses about 25% of his or her muscle mass. By age 90, another 25% has disappeared. The nerves that signal muscles to contract also can deteriorate with age. At the same time, fat tends to accumulate around muscle fibers, which can lead to mobility problems.

Sarcopenia poses a major threat to the independence of older adults. But while some muscle loss seems to be an inevitable part of aging (because it gets harder to build muscle as you get older), much can be done to halt or slow the decline. Resistance training can boost muscle strength and also reduce the amount of fat that accumulates around muscles. Even elderly people can prevent a great deal of muscle loss with a strength training program.

In fact, it's likely that the problem of declining muscle strength stems from lack of use as much as the inevitable changes that accompany age. Maintaining your muscles is one of the most important steps you can take to ensure your mobility and independence in later life.

Building a strength training routine

Building your muscles through strength training can improve mobility at all ages and fitness levels. If you're already physically fit, boosting your muscle workout can help you maintain your muscle mass and performance as you age. If you have lost some of your mobility, strength training may help you regain it—allowing you to use a cane instead of a walker, for instance, or maintain your walking speed for a longer period of time. It can help you accomplish tasks like lifting grocery bags or getting in and out of a car.

To get the full benefits of strength training, you have to make it a routine—and keep it up over time—because the benefits disappear when you stop exercising. The most important factor in choosing any exercise routine is designing something you'll be able to do regularly for the long haul. The goal is to maintain your muscles, not to build a new physique: aim for comfort, safety, and consistency, and go for more repetitions with less weight to build stamina. Check with your doctor before embarking on a strength training program if you have a heart condition, a previous injury, or any chronic diseases that could potentially be exacerbated by exercise.

There are endless ways to exercise effectively, so pick the approach that works best for you. The exercises described in this chapter (see "Strengthening exercises for mobility and power," page 25) can be performed on your own with minimal equipment. Many people choose to work out at home because it's convenient, fits into any schedule, and avoids membership costs of a gym. You can do much with a set of handheld weights, ankle cuffs with adjustable weight bars, a nonslip mat, and a sturdy chair.

Other people prefer the structure of a gym, or even working with a personal trainer for motivation. If you have a health condition or are recovering from an injury, consider seeing a physiatrist or physical therapist who can set you up with exercises that are safe and beneficial for your condition. If you work with a personal trainer, ask about his or her certification—the American College of Sports Medicine offers the most rigorous certification program. Make sure the trainer respects your body's capabilities and

Hip extension

Exercises the muscles of the buttocks and back thighs

While wearing ankle weights, stand 12 inches behind a sturdy chair. Holding on to the back of the chair for balance, bend your trunk forward 45 degrees. Slowly raise your right leg straight out behind you. Lift it as high as possible without bending your knee. Pause. Slowly lower the leg. Do this eight to 12 times. Repeat with your left leg. Rest and repeat on both sides.

Chair stand

Exercises the muscles of the abdomen, hips, front thighs, and buttocks

Place a sturdy chair in such a way that the back of it is resting against a wall. Sit at the front of the chair, knees bent, feet flat on the floor and slightly apart. Keeping your back and shoulders straight, stand up slowly, using your hands as little as possible. Slowly sit back down. Aim for eight to 12 repetitions. Rest and repeat the entire set.

Power move: Change the move slightly for the last set by rising from the chair quickly. Sit down again at a normal pace.

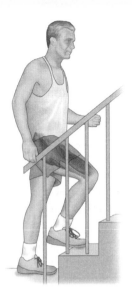

Stair climbing

Exercises the muscles of the front thighs and buttocks

Holding on to the handrail for balance if necessary, walk up and down a flight of at least 10 stairs at a pace that feels comfortable. Pause at the top only if you need to do so. Rest when you reach the bottom. Repeat four times.

Power move: If your balance is good, go up the stairs as briskly as you can and down at your normal pace for the last set.

---

limits; people can end up with injuries working with trainers who push too hard.

Aging and power training

Just as muscle mass and strength decline with age, so does muscle power, which represents the combination of strength and speed. Faced with a four-lane intersection, you may have enough strength to walk across the street. But can you cross all four lanes of traffic before the light changes? Power, not just strength, can get you from one side to the other safely. Likewise, by helping you react swiftly if you start to trip or lose your balance, power can actually prevent falls.

The goal of strength training is to challenge your muscles to the point of exhaustion. The goal of power training is to accomplish tasks more quickly and effectively. There's no need to lift extra weight, which could cause a muscle strain or other injury. Instead, lower the amount of resistance you would normally use for typical strength training exercises, such as biceps curls, and focus on quick movements (see two examples in the "Strengthening exercises," above). Another option is to wear a weighted vest, to create some additional challenge to power moves. You can also practice power in your daily activities by climbing a staircase rapidly or rising quickly from a chair.

Strengthening your core

The classic core exercise is a front plank, which exercises and strengthens all your core muscles. But if you have mobility problems, you will probably want to start with the modified version below, leaning on a countertop.

Front plank on countertop ▼
Wearing nonskid, rubber-soled shoes, stand facing a countertop with your feet together. Tighten your abdominal muscles and lower your upper body weight onto your forearms on the counter. Clasp your hands together and align your shoulders directly over your elbows. Step back on the balls of your feet until you are balancing your body in a line. Hold for 15 to 60 seconds. Rest and repeat.

Tips and techniques:
• Keep your head and spine neutral during the plank.
• Keep your shoulders down and back.
• Breathe comfortably.

Front plank ▼
Start on your hands and knees. Tighten your abdominal muscles and lower your upper body onto your forearms, clasping your hands together and aligning your shoulders directly over your elbows. Extend both legs with your feet flexed and toes touching the floor so that you balance your body in a line like a plank. Hold for 15 to 60 seconds. Then rest for 30 to 60 seconds and repeat.

Functional exercises

Functional exercises can help protect or improve mobility. These exercises mimic daily activities—carrying a heavy object across the room, for instance, or squatting to pick up an object from a low shelf. The benefit of these exercises is they directly target the activities you're already likely doing; the trade-off is that it's more difficult to target specific muscle groups and to incrementally build your strength. Functional exercises may be part of a strength training or rehabilitation program, but you can look for ways to do your own exercises at home.

Look for activities that challenge you in strength, power, balance, or flexibility, and set up a way to repeat the movement in sets. Use small hand weights or everyday objects like a book or bag of groceries to add a challenge. In this way, you can supplement any exercise routine with small daily activities. One of the best functional exercises is simply walking up and down stairs. If you have the opportunity to take the stairs instead of an escalator or elevator, do it.

A strong core

Exercises that strengthen your body's core are also essential for maintaining mobility and independence, including the ability to carry out basic tasks such as bending to pick up a package or carrying a bag of groceries. The core isn't just your abdomen; it includes muscles of the back, sides, pelvis, and buttocks. These muscles are involved in some way in almost everything you do. They even help you stand straight or sit up in a chair. If you have weakness or imbalance in the core muscles, it can lead to back pain, poor posture, and overall weakness, and the effects can spill over into other parts of the body, creating an uneven gait, joint misalignments, balance problems, and a susceptibility to injuries and falls.

Because your core muscles are vital to many kinds of movements, you engage them when you do many types of exercise. But adding some core-focused exercises, like front planks (at left) can help you target core muscles. If the standard plank is too difficult, try the "front plank on countertop" exercise. Unlike sit-ups and crunches, which isolate a few abdominal muscles, planks work all the core muscles at once. ▼

Balancing act

Young, healthy adults may be aware of their sense of balance only when doing something that strongly challenges it, like standing on one leg in a yoga class or hopping on rocks across a stream. The fact that most of us don't think much about balance is a testament to how deeply ingrained and instinctive our balance systems are.

In reality, our bodies are engaged in a constant battle with gravity to keep from falling over. Actions as simple as sitting upright in a chair or walking across the room require several sensory systems working together to sense your body's position in space, as well as nerves and muscles to adeptly shift position as needed to keep you upright. Static balance is the ability to hold a position like standing still, and active balance enables you to think ahead to know where to position yourself to execute a movement smoothly.

With aging, the acuity of these systems gradually declines. In adulthood and particularly old age, falls and stumbles can bring more severe consequences.

Falls can lead to injuries that have lasting consequences for mobility, such as hip fractures. That's why maintaining balance and avoiding falls is a crucial part of remaining active and mobile.

The body's balance system

Balance is not controlled by one separate system in the body. Instead, it is the result of a network of systems working together.

The vestibular system. The key to your sense of balance is the vestibular system in the inner ear (see Figure 8, below). Problems with the vestibular system can result in vertigo, a sensation of moving or spinning even though you aren't. The vestibular system consists of two main components. The first consists of the three semicircular canals, ringlike structures that are oriented in different directions, with each one at right angles to the other two. The canals are filled with a thick fluid that moves as the inner ear tilts. Specialized cells called

---

Figure 8: The outer, middle, and inner ear

The outer ear consists of the parts you can see: the fleshy outer part (called the auricle), the ear canal, and the eardrum.

The middle ear is an air-filled cavity containing the ossicles, three small bones (malleus, incus, and stapes) that transmit vibrations to the inner ear.

The inner ear is a complex system of membranous canals protected by a bony casing. Inside, the spiral-shaped cochlea contains the hair cells that transmit sound to the auditory nerve, which conducts sound to the brain.

The vestibular system, which regulates balance, is also part of the inner ear and includes the three semicircular canals known as the labyrinth, filled with a thick fluid that moves as the inner ear tilts. Special cells sense this movement.

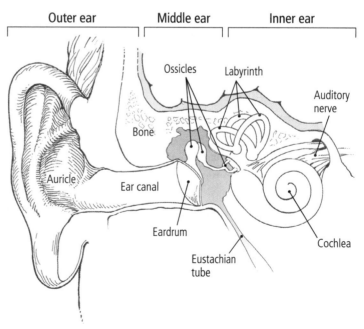

hair cells sense the movement of this fluid and send signals through the acoustic nerve to the brain. The unique arrangement of the canals means that each is sensitive to different directions of movement; together, they tell the brain about the position of the head and any rotational movements it makes through space.

The other part of the vestibular system includes two other structures called the utricle and saccule, together known as the otolith organs. They are pouches lined with hair cells embedded in a layer of gel, above which is a membrane containing calcium carbonate crystals. When you tilt your head, the pull of gravity on the crystals causes them to move, pulling on the hair cells in the gel below, which relay a signal to the brain letting it know the position and tilt of the head. The utricle also senses horizontal head movements, such as when you're moving forward, and the saccule senses the vertical force of gravity and vertical accelerations, such as when you stand up.

Proprioception and touch. Proprioception is the ability to know where the different parts of your body are in space—whether your legs are straight or bent, whether your arms are down at your sides or over your head, whether you're standing on one leg or lying on your back. It's accomplished through nerves that are distributed throughout the body in muscles, tendons, and joints. Collectively, the information from these nerves informs your brain about what your body is doing, and the brain responds by adjusting the position of the body to maintain balance. Added to this internal sense of your body's placement are the external sensations you feel—the pressure of the ground below your feet or your back resting against a chair—which also give you cues about how to position your body.

Vision. Most of us rely on vision to maintain balance. (Try standing on one leg with your eyes closed, and you'll see how much harder it is than performing the same exercise with your eyes open.) Vision is also important for assessing changes in your surroundings as you move. By looking at the ground ahead of you, for instance, you can anticipate where to place your foot to keep from tripping on a rock or slipping on a curb. (For more on vision's role in mobility, see "Vision," page 31.)

Nerves and the spinal cord. All of these sensory systems collect information about your body and its environment that is transmitted to the brain; nerves also relay your brain's commands back to the body, allowing you to quickly respond to whatever new sensations you're perceiving. Your spinal cord is the information superhighway that channels all this two-way traffic. The spinal cord is also able to initiate reflexes—quick responses to stimuli that don't require the brain's instructions. Reflexes can be important for catching yourself before falling if you're suddenly knocked off balance.

Balance and aging

Keeping your body in balance requires marshaling information from different senses, but the sensory information coming in can diminish with age. That

▶ **Blood pressure and fainting**

As the heart ages, its ability to pump faster when challenged, such as during exercise, gradually decreases. That's why a treadmill at the gym lists different target and maximum heart rates for different ages. Something as simple as standing up also puts a similar challenge on the heart. When you stand up after sitting in a chair, about half a quart of blood plummets downward toward the lower body. A healthy heart compensates for this by speeding up to pump more blood to the brain. If that doesn't happen, there's a sudden drop in blood pressure called postural hypotension. Some people feel it as a mild "head rush" when standing that quickly goes away, but because older adults have a harder time raising their heart rate, they may have more dramatic symptoms: dizziness, light-headedness, and even fainting.

Postural hypotension can be caused by dehydration, prolonged bed rest, cholesterol-clogged arteries, and diabetes. Some medications used to treat high blood pressure can worsen the problem. For some older adults, just eating a meal can cause dizziness or fainting upon getting up from the table because blood is being sent to the stomach and intestines to aid digestion.

Dizzy spells and fainting can lead to injuries and falls. People who are susceptible to postural hypotension should always rise slowly and carefully after sitting or lying down, avoid getting dehydrated, and take care not to eat meals too quickly.

poses a challenge for coordination and balance. Visual acuity—the ability to see objects clearly and in focus—wanes with age, as does night vision, depth perception, and the ability to see contrast between light and dark. Proprioception can also become weaker with age, particularly in people who have damage to the peripheral nerves because of diabetes or another medical condition.

The combination of reduced sensations, declines in muscle strength, and other age-related health problems (see "Blood pressure and fainting," page 28) puts people at increasingly greater risk of falling as they age. Falls are the leading cause of death from injury in people over age 65. Each year, one in three people in this age group has a fall.

Falls are the primary cause of broken hips, which pose a serious threat to future mobility. They can also lead to other injuries to the feet, ankles, knees, or back that require a long recovery period. Injuries to the upper body—like the hands, shoulders, or face—can also keep you from performing day-to-day tasks independently. A fall that leaves relatively minor physical injuries can still injure your confidence, making you less likely to exercise and move around on your own. Fear of falling again can have a negative impact on your physical and emotional health, keeping you away from activities you enjoy and making you feel more isolated.

If you experience a fall or a stumble, take it as an opportunity to assess your health and think about taking steps to improve your balance and coordination, or to reduce your risk of falling again by modifying your home (see "Adapting and fall-proofing your home," page 43) or your routine.

Health conditions that affect balance

In addition to age-related changes, some common health conditions can interfere with balance and coordination, posing challenges for movement—and medications for many conditions can cause problems (see "Medications and balance," above right).

Vestibular disorders. The inner ear structures of the vestibular system can be temporarily or permanently disrupted because of injury, allergies, infec-

---

Medications and balance

A long list of medications can affect balance and raise the risk of falling, mostly because of their potential to cause side effects like dizziness, drowsiness, confusion, or fainting. As people get older they tend to take multiple medications, which can cause a greater number or intensity of side effects; taking four or more medications at once is associated with a higher risk of falling. Some types of drugs that can cause problems are

- psychiatric drugs such as antipsychotics, tricyclic antidepressants, and anti-anxiety drugs
- anticholinergic/antispasmodic drugs
- muscle relaxants
- antihistamines
- pain medications such as opioids and nonsteroidal anti-inflammatory drugs (NSAIDs)
- heart drugs, such as anti-arrhythmics, vasodilators, and digoxin.

Not all of these will cause problems for all people. Alert your doctor to any side effects you feel that could put you at risk of falls or injuries. Your doctor can help you weigh the risks of the medication or adopt strategies to manage the side effects.

---

tions, blood circulation problems, or other disease processes. Vestibular disorders require treatment, which can include balance rehabilitation exercises, medications, and surgery.

Strokes. Strokes are a major cause of mobility loss, and balance can be affected too, through loss of sensation or movement on one side of the body, loss of coordination, weakness, numbness, or vision loss. Strokes can also cause cognitive impairments that make it harder to concentrate, a necessary skill for navigating challenging terrain.

Movement disorders. Parkinson's disease can cause balance-disturbing tremors, rigidity of the legs and torso, slowness of movements, and difficulty coordinating movements.

Peripheral neuropathy. Damage to the peripheral nerves in the arms, legs, feet, and hands can cause tingling, numbness, muscle weakness, or pain that hampers smooth movement. Diabetes is a key cause of this kind of nerve damage. It can also result from injury, alcoholism, or infection.

Balance exercises

Muscles and bones need to be challenged or else they deteriorate. The same is true of balance. Fortunately, balance and coordination can be maintained with practice and even improve over time.

Many types of physical activity challenge the balance system. If you do yoga, dance, or tai chi, you're giving your balance system a workout by putting your body in challenging positions. However, if most of your exercise is using a stationary bike or weight machines, or simply walking on a path, you may be missing out on a chance to build up your balance abilities along with your muscles and cardiovascular fitness. Here are two targeted exercises you can do at home to challenge and improve your balance.

Heel-to-toe walk ►

Position your heel just in front of the toes of the opposite foot as you walk forward for eight to 12 steps. Heel and toes should actually touch each time you take a step. If necessary, steady yourself by putting one hand on a counter as you walk at first, and then work toward doing this without support. Repeat two to four times.

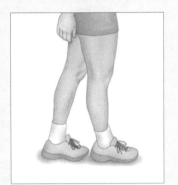

Single leg stance ▼

Stand on one foot for up to 30 seconds. Put your foot down and repeat on the opposite side. Perform two to four times on each leg. If this is too hard, steady yourself by holding on to the back of a chair at first, then work toward doing this without support. For an added challenge, you can add ankle weights.

Excess weight. Overweight and obesity can throw off balance and make you more prone to falling. People who are obese are also more likely to become disabled after a fall.

Reducing the risk of falls

To what extent can falls be prevented? This topic has been an important target of research. In brief, many direct interventions to prevent falls seem to be helpful. These include exercises to improve muscle strength, balance, and gait; physical therapy; and taking 800 IU of vitamin D a day. The American Geriatrics Society also recommends programs that help people assess and modify the safety of their homes and improve their ability to perform daily tasks safely.

The first step toward keeping yourself or a loved one from falling is to know when there's a problem. Look for these warning signs:

- difficulty climbing stairs without leaning heavily on a rail
- fatigue when performing basic tasks like housework

- leaning on furniture to cross a room
- hesitancy walking and negotiating steps and uneven surfaces
- requiring more assistance getting in and out of chairs, a car, or a shower or bath
- changes in gait—excessive slowness, favoring one side over another, shuffling
- fear of falling (paradoxically, people who are afraid of falls become increasingly hesitant and sedentary, which only weakens their bodies and puts them at further risk)
- avoiding bathing, changing clothes, or other basic tasks, because of fear of falls or injuries.

If you notice any of these, a conversation with a doctor is in order. A physical therapist or other clinician can create a program to reduce your fall risk. This includes exercises to build strength, improve your sense of balance, increase your activity level, and build your confidence to allow you to overcome a fear of falling. Some clinical programs also include a home visit to assess whether you can make changes to your home to help prevent falls (see "Adapting and fall-proofing your home," page 43). ▼

The mind and senses: Staying sharp

Mobility requires more than just bones, muscles, tendons, and cartilage. It requires being able to assess your environment so you can move through it safely and effectively. To get from point A to point B, you must know where point B is, whether there are any steps or rough terrain between them, and what movements your body needs to accomplish to reach your goal. And that's just the movements that your own body performs; put that body into a car, and the skills you need change. When driving, you need to sense and respond to fast-moving traffic and navigate complex routes. If you're moving through your own neighborhood or city, you must access your memories of the streets, and if you're driving in unfamiliar places, you must locate and respond to street signs and other directional cues (see "Driving: Staying up to the challenge," page 33).

Vision

Humans are visual animals. Although people who are visually impaired or even completely blind can learn to move around adeptly by using other senses, the rest of us rely heavily on our vision for all our day-to-day tasks, and vision is the sense that most people are most afraid of losing. Age-related vision loss can dramatically limit your daily activities. And if you deal with any other challenges to your mobility, such as arthritis, a longstanding injury, or chronic pain, vision loss can add to the challenges those conditions already pose. Yet many people do not think about the health of their eyes or seek out

medical attention for vision problems that develop with aging until the problem is severe.

The visual system undergoes many changes with age. In particular, the lens inside the eye grows harder, which can cause presbyopia, an inability to clearly distinguish close objects, such as the printed words of a book. Even changes that seem cosmetic can affect vision; muscles in the face shrink, while skin gets thinner and begins to sag—and sagging eyelids and weakening muscles can interfere with normal vision.

While such changes are part of normal aging, others could signal a vision-related disease. The following conditions are the most common causes of vision impairment.

Figure 9: Lens replacement surgery for cataracts

1.

Incision

Clouded lens

The ophthalmologist makes a small incision about an eighth of an inch long in the side of the cornea.

2.

Phacoemulsifier

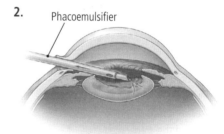

Using a small, needle-like probe called a phacoemulsifier, the doctor directs high-frequency sound waves through the lens to break it into small pieces, which are then gently suctioned out through the probe.

3.

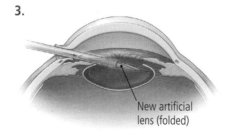

New artificial lens (folded)

The artificial lens, which is folded to fit inside the probe, is inserted through the same incision.

4.

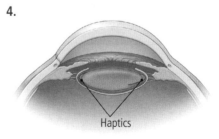

Haptics

The new lens unfolds inside the lens capsule and is held in place by tiny loops called haptics.

Cataract. The lens of the eye can become cloudy over time, a condition known as a cataract. Cataracts are extremely common; most people over age 60 have some cloudiness of the lens, and about half of people ages 65 to 74 and 70% of those 75 and older have cataracts. Cataracts develop slowly, so you may not realize you're experiencing symptoms at first. Objects may look slightly blurry or dim, and your eyes may be sensitive to the glare of bright lights. You may become more nearsighted or begin to notice a lessening in your ability to see colors and to see at night.

Age is the biggest risk factor, but you're more likely to get cataracts if you have a family history of cataracts or if you smoke, drink alcohol excessively, have had an eye injury, use corticosteroid medications, have diabetes, or are obese. An eye doctor can look for cataracts by dilating the pupils and using a slit lamp to check the interior of the eyes.

At the early stage of cataracts, be proactive about giving yourself the best possible conditions to aid your vision. Change your eyeglass or contact prescription if needed, keep your house or workspace well-lit, and make sure your computer monitor is positioned so that there isn't glare from overhead lights or windows (you can also install an anti-glare screen on your monitor). Use eyeglasses with an antireflective coating on the lenses.

The only proven treatment for cataracts is lens replacement surgery (see Figure 9, page 31). This involves taking out the cloudy lens in your eye and replacing it with a clear artificial lens, called an intraocular lens. It is an extremely common and safe procedure; it can now be performed on an outpatient basis under local anesthesia, without a hospital stay. Some people never need it, while others can safely delay it for months or years, or have surgery in one eye but not the other. But while avoiding an invasive procedure is appealing, it's important not to delay or avoid surgery if you're having vision problems that interfere with your daily activities, inhibit your independence, or threaten your safety.

Glaucoma. Glaucoma is a condition that damages the optic nerve, which relays information from the eye's retina to the brain. This damage can result in vision loss or blindness. Although it can occur in anyone, it's more common in people over 60, African Americans, Mexican Americans, and people with a family history of glaucoma. Other conditions—such as diabetes, high blood pressure, and severe nearsightedness or farsightedness—can also increase the risk of developing glaucoma.

The most common type of the disease, called open-angle glaucoma, is caused by poor drainage of aqueous humor (the fluid in the eye), leading to a backup of the fluid and a gradual but persistent elevation of pressure inside the eye. Eventually, this pressure causes nerve cells to die or blood vessels to be cut off, beginning with tiny nerve fibers affecting peripheral vision but gradually closing in until central vision is lost as well. However, other factors in addition to high intraocular pressure also seem to play a role in promoting the death of nerve cells, since not everyone with high pressure in the eye gets glaucoma.

By the time you begin to notice visual disturbances (often poor peripheral vision, blind spots, or difficulty

Figure 10: Laser trabeculoplasty for glaucoma

In this procedure, the surgeon uses a high-energy beam of light (laser) to produce small burns on the trabecular meshwork. The procedure improves the flow of aqueous humor out of the eye, thus lowering intraocular pressure. A slit-lamp microscope and a special contact lens allow the ophthalmologist to get a detailed view of the angle where the iris, cornea, and sclera meet, and to focus the laser on the tissue.

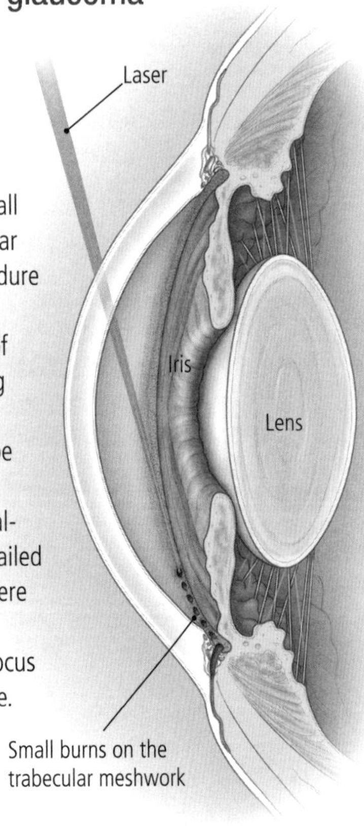

Laser

Iris

Lens

Small burns on the trabecular meshwork

Driving: Staying up to the challenge

For many people, driving a car is a key part of maintaining independence, particularly if they live in places without easy public transportation. If you're like many people, you wonder how long you will be able to keep driving.

Driving requires coordination of the senses, brain, and body. Several age-related changes can affect your ability to drive safely. The most obvious is vision problems like trouble with near and far vision, night vision, peripheral vision, and sensitivity to contrast and glare. If you need glasses or contact lenses, use them when you drive and keep your prescription up to date. Loss of night vision can't be corrected with glasses, but you could consider adding an anti-glare coating to your eyeglasses to reduce the temporary blindness caused by oncoming headlights. Age-related eye diseases such as macular degeneration, presbyopia, glaucoma, and cataract can affect driving ability, so make sure to have regular eye exams to catch these early. Cataracts, for example, make night driving particularly difficult, but can be fixed with cataract surgery. People who have cataract surgery have a greatly reduced risk of driving-related difficulties and motor vehicle accidents than people with cataracts who don't have surgery.

Measures that may help

Making adjustments to your car is one way to cope with challenges driving. These include installing wider side- and rear-view mirrors to give better visibility and making sure your dashboard lights are at their brightest setting. Many older drivers need to make lifestyle adjustments as well, such as avoiding driving in the rain, at night, or during rush hour, and steering clear of high-traffic routes.

To help you stay on top of your driving skills, think about taking one of the courses offered for older drivers by either AARP (www.aarp.org/families/driver_safety) or alternately AAA (www.seniordrivers.org). These courses cover everything from loss of vision, hearing, cognitive function, and motor function to the side effects of common medications.

A deterioration in thinking skills or memory can also affect your ability to remember routes, pay attention to traffic, react to changes, and make decisions. And physical problems such as arthritis, muscle weakness, or nerve damage can affect how well you can control your vehicle. Talk with your doctor about these concerns and take the steps you can to protect your vision, reflexes, and mental sharpness, but be aware that some age-related problems can't be halted.

At some point, older people need to make tough decisions about whether to stop driving. Based on current life expectancies, most older drivers will outlive their ability to drive by several years. An objective assessment can help with this decision. Older drivers can get a comprehensive driving assessment from an occupational therapist, who can determine whether they can continue to drive safely, and may recommend modifications, restrictions, or rehabilitation and training.

---

adjusting to the dark), the disease has already become severe. A doctor can detect glaucoma before you notice it, which makes regular checkups important. For open-angle glaucoma, treatment usually begins with topical medications—eye drops or sometimes ointments—administered one to several times a day. Depending on the severity of the condition, multiple drops and sometimes pills may be required. Most ophthalmologists begin with the lowest effective dose to minimize cost and potential side effects. Should medicines fail to control pressure, surgery may be necessary (see Figure 10, page 32).

Age-related macular degeneration. Age-related macular degeneration (AMD) is another slowly progressing disease. It affects one of the most important places in the eye for vision—the macula, a bundle of cells at the center of the retina responsible for sharp central vision. There are two forms of the condition:

Dry AMD, the more common form, is caused by thinning of the retina and loss of photoreceptor cells.

Wet AMD is less common but more serious. It occurs when abnormal blood vessels grow into the retina and cause a marked loss of central vision.

AMD is most common in people over 60, though it can occur earlier. As in glaucoma, symptoms often appear late in the disease process, but the vision loss is different. You may notice a blurred spot in the center of your vision that can progress to blank spots; also, sometimes objects appear less bright. AMD does not cause total blindness, but at later stages it can hamper your mobility and independence by making it difficult to drive, read, use computers or smartphones, or do work and activities that involve seeing things up close.

Although age is the biggest risk factor for AMD, smoking more than doubles your risk; Caucasians and people with a family history of AMD are also at higher risk of developing the disease. The only current treatment for dry AMD is dietary supplementa-

▶ Choosing sunglasses

A good way to protect your vision is to wear sunglasses that help block ultraviolet (UV) rays of the sun. In addition to its well-known effects on skin, UV light can cause growths on the eye surface and boost the risk of developing cataracts and macular degeneration.

Wearing sunglasses also makes vision more comfortable by reducing visible light, which makes it easier for you to navigate your environment. Look for glasses that are labeled as blocking at least 99% of the two different kinds of ultraviolet rays, UVA and UVB. Or choose glasses labeled "UV400," which block all UVA and UVB radiation and other potentially harmful rays. Polarized lenses don't block UV rays, but they can reduce glare from reflective light when you're driving or spending time on the water.

Another consideration is the shape of the lenses. Small lenses allow a lot of light through the sides of the glasses, which can undo their benefit. Glasses that are larger and wrap around the eyes offer more protection. Wearing a hat is also important to reduce the amount of sun that your glasses have to block.

All people should protect their eyes from UV rays, but it's especially important for people who already have eye disease or have had cataract surgery. In addition, certain antibiotics and other drugs, like amiodarone (Cordarone), make the eyes more sensitive to light, so people who take these medications should be especially vigilant about wearing sunglasses.

tion with a formulation of antioxidants that has been shown to be beneficial. Wet AMD is treated with anti-VEGF drugs, which inhibit the growth of new blood vessels in the eye.

Diabetic and hypertensive retinopathy. High blood sugar—the hallmark of diabetes—and high blood pressure both damage small blood vessels in the retina. Over time, this leads to vision loss and blindness. Although there is no cure for the condition, treatments using laser therapies and medications can help slow the damage and prevent blindness. Working to control blood sugar and blood pressure can keep vision loss at bay. Having yearly eye exams that include a retina check is also important.

Living with vision problems

The most important step to living successfully with vision problems is recognizing them. Too often, peo-ple either ignore or deny changes to their vision. That can keep them from adapting successfully and, if the vision loss is severe, can put themselves or others in harm's way. Many people make do with low vision. Yet there are ways to cope, and many devices and products are available to help you. Taking steps to stay active and connected in spite of low vision will ensure that the rest of your health doesn't suffer.

An ophthalmologist, optometrist, or rehabilitation specialist can help you develop strategies to cope with low vision. Focus on what could be changed in your daily environment to make it easier for you to see important objects. One strategy is to create contrasts—make sure that stairs, doors, or objects you need to find stand out from their surroundings, either with bright colors or differences in shade. You'll see white pills better if you place them on a dark tablecloth, and placing brightly colored tape on the stairs and on handles of doors and appliances can help you distinguish them. You may need brighter lights than before, particularly when reading.

Magnifying lenses, either incorporated into eyeglass lenses, held in the hand, or mounted on a stand, can help you do close work like reading or sewing. Similarly, magnifying mirrors can help with shaving or applying cosmetics. An e-reader, such as a Kindle, allows you to adjust the size of the type, and many software programs and apps will also enlarge text on a screen. There are even text-to-speech programs that can read text on a screen aloud to you. No single product can compensate for low vision. Instead, try different task-specific tools to accomplish the activities that matter to you. The key is to have patience with yourself. Learning to use magnifying lenses and other aids is like learning to walk with crutches—it may require some effort and adjustment to learn to accomplish tasks easily, but adopting the new habits can help you maintain your everyday activities.

Preserving eye health

Vision changes and eye diseases are common consequences of aging, but they're not inevitable. It's estimated that as much as 40% to 50% of all blindness could be avoided with proper treatment and preventive measures.

The most important step toward keeping eyes healthy is to get regular dilated eye exams, particularly if you have a personal or family history of eye disease. People who have had longstanding vision problems and require glasses and contacts usually have regular exams when they update their prescriptions, but other people may fail to think about their eye health. The American Academy of Ophthalmologists recommends an eye exam every two years for people at any age at high risk of eye disease, as well as everyone over age 65. But get any vision problems checked right away, and keep glasses or contact lenses updated with a current prescription.

Quitting or avoiding smoking is another important step to preserving eye health. Following a healthy lifestyle and managing chronic diseases such as diabetes and high blood pressure will ultimately benefit your vision. Diet also plays a role in eye health: diets rich in leafy green vegetables like collard greens, kale, and spinach, and fish high in omega-3 fatty acids, help protect vision.

Another way to safeguard your vision is to wear sunglasses when needed to protect your eyes from ultraviolet rays (see "Choosing sunglasses," page 34).

Hearing

If you've noticed problems with your hearing, you're not alone. About one-third of people in their 60s and more than 80% of those over 85 have some level of hearing loss—that's at least 28 million adults in the United States. Men tend to lose their hearing earlier than women and have more severe hearing loss. Some hearing loss is related to a physical obstruction of the ear canal by earwax, debris, inflammation, or fluid. But most hearing loss is caused by damage to the sensory hair cells in the ear or the nerves that transmit auditory signals to the brain.

Presbycusis, or age-related hearing loss, is the leading cause of hearing problems. Besides age, other factors that contribute to hearing loss are exposure to loud noise, smoking, various diseases, and exposure to some medications or chemicals.

It may not be obvious that hearing loss can harm independence, since we use our eyes to get around much more than we use our ears. But it can, and does. In particular, in recent years, it has come to light that protecting and treating hearing loss not only preserves and restores your hearing, but also protects your brain from decline and possibly even from dementia. The reasons for this association are not yet known. One possibility is that when people struggle with their hearing, they often withdraw from social interactions with family and friends, which leads to depression. This isolation in itself is a known risk factor for dementia. Another possibility is that a decline in hearing accelerates a decline in brain function in areas related to auditory processing, with "cascading consequences" for neural processes that support perception and cognition.

Treating hearing loss

Age-related hearing loss is often a gradual process, and you may adjust to incremental changes without noticing them—in fact, only 20% of people over 65 with hearing loss that is moderate to profound believe that they have a hearing problem. People often lose the ability to hear some frequencies of sound rather than all sounds. It's common to first find it difficult to hear high-frequency sounds like a hiss or whisper, or sounds like "s" and "th" and "f" in speech. You may have trouble hearing certain sounds at low volumes, notice a lack of clarity, or feel you can hear the words people say but can't understand them. The problem is usually most obvious in situations with background noise, like when you're trying to have a conversation at a restaurant or you're watching TV with a fan running in the background.

Age-related hearing loss does not necessarily require treatment, but it's still important to have your hearing tested by an audiologist if you suspect you're not hearing as well as you used to, and to have any hearing loss monitored. It may result from a treatable condition like wax or fluid buildup. If the hearing loss is mild, an audiologist can recommend strategies to keep it from interfering with conversations or activities.

If your hearing loss is serious enough to require a hearing aid, the good news is that technological advancements have made hearing aids smaller and better with less distortion. There are many choices in the size and shape of the hearing aids, as well as features like reducing background noise, amplifying selective sounds, and connecting wirelessly to a cellphone. Talk to your audiologist about what type is best suited to your hearing loss, lifestyle, and budget.

Preventing hearing loss

To prevent hearing loss, turn down the volume. Loud noise can destroy specialized cells in the ears that sense sound. It's not just rock concerts that hurt hearing; leaf and snow blowers, lawn mowers, chain saws, wood chippers, and even loud appliances in the home like hair dryers can cause damage. Use earplugs or earmuffs if you're going to be hearing loud noises. If you listen to music on headphones or earbuds, be aware that both the volume and the length of time you're listening make a difference. Keep the volume low, and don't turn it up to drown out background noise (invest in noise-canceling headphones instead).

Mobility and your brain

The brain is the master controller of movement, so it's not surprising that changes in brain function can cause problems with mobility. Taking care of your brain is part and parcel of staying mobile as you age, as well as avoiding further declines in physical health if you're living with a chronic condition. Mobility is linked to a few different brain functions.

Attention. Almost every mental task involves some degree of attention—focusing on one object or aspect of your environment and not others. Older adults sometimes have difficulty dividing and switching their attention (though they are generally better at sustaining attention on a single task compared with younger adults). This can make it hard to accomplish tasks that put complex demands on the brain and senses, like navigating a crowded airport or driving a car. Declines in attention are linked to gait changes and susceptibility to injuries and falls.

Executive function. The ability to make plans, organize your schedule and life, manage your time, behave and speak appropriately, and adapt your behavior based on past experiences are all part of a

▶ Gait and cognition

Doctors used to consider physical abilities separately from mental abilities when they evaluated older patients. But increasingly, there's been a realization that how you walk (which tells a doctor about your physical health and risk of falls) changes when there is a decline in how well your brain accomplishes certain tasks.

It's long been appreciated that people with dementia have a greater risk of falls. And falls can be particularly devastating to this population: people who have cognitive problems are five times more likely to require institutional care than people who fall but are in good cognitive health. Interventions designed to prevent falls (using balance training and other techniques) have had less success in people with dementia.

set of skills often referred to collectively as "executive function." As the name implies, these are high-level skills that help you control your life and manage social situations—think of them as your ability to be your own boss. Declines in executive function are linked to mobility problems and falls.

Working memory. Working memory is the ability to hold information you just learned in your mind for a short time and manipulating that information. Loss of working memory has been linked to a slower gait in older adults and may reflect a general difficulty devoting brain power to complex tasks (see "Gait and cognition," above).

Mood and motivation. Your mood and feelings of motivation can affect mobility. People with chronic depression are more likely than others to have a decline in thinking skills and memory, which have been linked to trouble getting around. Staying mobile and independent also requires motivation. Anything that reduces your motivation to get out and about, from a stroke-related brain injury to depression, can affect how motivated you are to be active, take on physical challenges, and cope with health problems.

Keeping your brain healthy

Science still has much to learn about the aging brain and how to ward off mental decline. But the following actions have consistently been linked to better brain functioning with age.

Stay physically active. Exercise can improve mental function in people with mild declines in thinking skills and memory.

Manage medical conditions. High blood pressure, high cholesterol, obesity, diabetes, hearing loss, and hormonal changes can lead to declines in thinking skills and memory. By keeping these conditions under control, you can help avoid the negative feedback loop between poor physical health, mental decline, and diminished mobility.

Check your medications. Many medications have side effects that can cloud the brain, including prescription medications to treat depression, overactive bladder, heartburn, and more. Even common over-the-counter drugs for allergies and colds can make you feel sleepy and confused. Many people take multiple medications, which can cause side effects to be more pronounced than from one drug alone.

Exercise your brain. Mental challenges can help keep the brain healthy and contribute to overall health. For you, that might involve reading, taking classes, writing in a journal, doing crossword puzzles, playing chess, participating in a book club or discussion group, taking on a volunteer position, or mastering a new hobby. But the most effective strategies are those that require the formation of new neural networks, such as learning a foreign language or taking up a new musical instrument. Whatever activities you choose, look for ways to engage mentally with new ideas, situations, or skills.

Get enough rest. Lack of sleep can cause confusion, forgetfulness, and fatigue. It has also been linked to weight gain, lowered immunity, and depression. Older people have more sleep-related problems, including insomnia (trouble falling asleep or staying asleep) and obstructive sleep apnea (briefly stopping breathing repeatedly during the night).

Stay social. Connections with others—whether they are family members, friends, neighbors, or people with a shared hobby—can help improve mental performance in older people. Social connections can also provide a buffer against the damaging effects of stress, depression, and anxiety. They are a key to remaining mobile and active. ◗

Is your diet sabotaging your mobility?

Your diet affects your ability to move and stay healthy in several ways. Your body depends on the nutrients in food to build bones, power muscle, repair and replace tissues, and keep your brain active and your heart pumping. The quality of your diet has a direct impact on how well your body can accomplish its myriad tasks. Epidemiological studies on older adults have linked low fruit and vegetable intake with higher risk of disability and correlated low levels of certain nutrients with higher rates of frailty.

Your diet also influences your risk of developing chronic diseases such as type 2 diabetes, heart disease, and osteoporosis, which have the potential to set you on a path of poor health and hinder your ability to live an active and independent life. So eating a healthy diet not only nourishes your body, it also helps to ensure that it remains free of disease.

Eating the right foods is important, but the amount of food you eat and how you balance the calories you take in with those you burn off also matter. Being overweight can make it more difficult to move easily in day-to-day activities, so the correlation between diet and mobility is very direct.

Keys to a healthy diet

Magazines, newspapers, and the Internet are filled with information—some great and some not-so-great—about how to eat right. Don't let the chatter confuse you; while the health benefits of various foods might be debated, the overall message of how to eat healthfully is surprisingly simple and consistent.

You can break it down into a few basic steps:

- Choose mostly plant-based foods that are unprocessed or minimally processed.
- Strive to eat a variety of fruits, vegetables, and whole grains over the course of the week, in order to ensure a balance of important nutrients.
- Eat only as much as you need, keeping your calorie intake and physical activity level in balance.

Of course, there are important details about the components of food—which foods are better for you than others, which nutrients you need most to keep your body healthy over time. But you don't need to worry too much about the details if you follow the basic principles above as a guide.

Thinkstock

With aging, however, there are additional challenges. A major problem for many people is that metabolism gradually slows with age, so the body requires fewer calories each day. Many people find it hard to cut back on the amount of food they eat, and they begin to gain weight. The same challenge faces people who have become less active because of disease, lost mobility, or disability. But while the need for calories declines, the need for important nutrients like protein, vitamins, and minerals stays the same. That means as you get older, it's even more important to make each meal count by choosing healthy, nutrient-rich foods rather than those full of "empty" calories.

While weighing too much is a growing problem among older adults, weighing too little can also be a cause for concern. Many older adults find that their appetite gradually declines. Eating too little can contribute to frailty and ill health, and it makes it more likely you will be undernourished. Making good choices about what you eat can help you have energy throughout the day and stay healthy for a long time.

Why unprocessed foods?

The first principle named earlier was to choose mostly plant-based foods that are unprocessed or minimally processed. Why? Supermarket shelves are filled with processed foods that claim to be health foods, but the healthiest choice is usually foods that are as close as possible to the way they came from nature. An actual apple, for instance, has lots of fiber, vitamins, minerals, and other nutrients. Process that apple into apple juice, and you lose fiber and some of those other nutrients. Turn the apple into a packaged fruit snack, and you get mostly sugar. The same goes for grains. Bread made entirely from whole grains is far better than bread made from refined flour—which is missing the outer casing and the inner germ of the nutrient-rich wheat berry. Whole, unprocessed grains are even better since they lack the added sugar and salt that bread usually has.

Real foods like fruits, vegetables, beans, nuts, and grains contain hundreds of nutrients. These nutrients, called phytochemicals or phytonutrients, work together and play important roles in health. Only some of them are added back to "fortified" processed foods. In addition, processed foods often contain extra sugar, fat, and salt to make them more tasty.

Processed foods are often a major part of the diet of older adults and people with mobility limitations because they are convenient, easy to store, and longer-lasting compared with fresh fruits and vegetables. But there are healthier ways to choose foods for convenience. Frozen fruits and vegetables, for instance, keep many of their nutrients without additives and can be easily defrosted and cooked or turned into a smoothie. And there are now many low-sodium versions of canned vegetables and beans, which make healthier choices. Instead of snacking on a granola bar that has lots of added sugars, you can snack on unsalted nuts, which have lots of protein, minerals, and "good" fats.

Building a healthy plate

To help you make healthy food choices, nutrition experts from the Harvard School of Public Health have devised the Healthy Eating Plate. It's a simple graphic that replaces the longstanding food pyramid that once imperfectly represented basic food groups in the diet. The Harvard Healthy Eating Plate (see Figure 11, page 40) gives detailed, evidence-based advice that can help you understand which foods should have a more prominent place in your diet, which ones you should avoid, and how to think about balancing foods in your diet for your overall health.

Fruits and vegetables. Fully half of the plate contains fruits and vegetables. That's because fruits and vegetables are high in important nutrients. They are mostly nutrient-dense without being calorie-dense, so they are an important part of your strategy to maximize nutrients in foods as you age. (Note that this plate doesn't count potatoes as vegetables because they contain a lot of starch, and so in the body they act more like white bread than a vegetable.) Diets high in fruits and vegetables can help lower blood pressure and reduce the risks of heart disease, stroke, eye disease, and probably some cancers. Eating fruits and vegetables also provides a good dose of fiber, which can help prevent or relieve constipation.

Aim to eat as much fresh produce as possible each day. Frozen fruits and vegetables are also a healthy option and easier to store and use when convenient. Canned vegetables are also good, though they often come with added sugars or salt. Look for low-sugar or low-sodium options when you do buy them. Dried fruit can add fiber and nutrients, but be care-ful—they deliver a lot of concentrated calories.

Whole grains. A quarter of the plate is whole grains. Grains provide inexpensive, easy calories. Most Americans get plenty of grains in their diet when you add up all the breakfast cereal, bread, pasta, rice, and various processed crackers and snacks. But most of these foods are full of rapidly digested carbohydrates that quickly boost blood sugar. Whole grains, in contrast, provide more slowly digested carbohydrates plus fiber, healthy fats, vitamins, minerals, plant enzymes, hormones, and hundreds of other phytochemicals. People who eat mostly whole grains are less likely to develop diabetes, have a heart attack or stroke, and die prematurely than people who eat mostly refined grains. Choosing whole grains over refined grains can also help curb appetite and improve cholesterol levels.

The key to making whole grains part of your lifestyle is to be adventurous. You can buy whole-grain versions of foods like breads, pizza dough, and pasta. You'll get even more of the benefits if you branch out to other kinds of intact grains: brown rice, quinoa, barley, polenta or grits, whole oats, bulgur (cracked wheat), and wild rice.

Protein. The final quarter is healthy sources of protein like fish, beans, soy products, nuts, seeds, poultry, eggs, and low-fat milk, cheese, yogurt, and other dairy foods. Try to limit red meat to no more than one to two servings per week. Avoid cured and processed meats like ham, hot dogs, and many lunch meats, choosing lean cuts of uncured meats instead. Eating a lot of cured or processed meats boosts the risk for heart disease, type 2 diabetes, colorectal cancer, and early death.

Explore plant sources of protein, which are a great way to get not only protein but also vitamins, minerals, fiber, and healthy fats. These include beans, chickpeas, edamame, split peas, lentils, nuts, and seeds.

Protein is particularly important for maintaining muscle strength with age. Although most

Figure 11: Harvard's Healthy Eating Plate

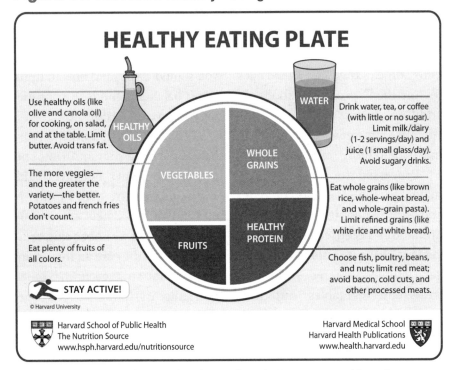

Sometimes a picture really is worth a thousand words. For a more nutritious diet, follow the guidelines on Harvard's Healthy Eating Plate.

Americans get more than enough protein in their diet, many older adults don't. Not eating enough protein can lead to age-related muscle loss (sarcopenia), a common condition that is responsible for frailty among many older adults (see "Masterful muscles," page 24). Eating lots of protein won't by itself keep your muscles strong—for that, you need to exercise. But without enough protein, your body can't replace or build muscle tissue.

It's a good idea to eat some protein with every meal or snack. Add some low-sodium canned beans or a hard-boiled egg to a salad, toss chopped nuts or seeds onto your cereal at breakfast, slather some peanut butter on an apple, pair nuts with carrot slices, or have a cup of plain low- or nonfat Greek yogurt with fruit.

Healthy fats. High-fat foods shouldn't be a major part of your plate, but there's no reason to ban fats from your diet. Instead, what's important is to choose fats that are better for health. "Good" fats—monounsaturated and polyunsaturated fats—can lower your risk of chronic disease; they are found in olive and other vegetable oils, nuts, seeds, and fish. "Bad" fats—saturated and trans fats—increase your disease risks and are found in red meat, butter, high-fat dairy products, and many processed foods.

Use healthy oils, like olive and canola, when cooking, in salad dressings, and at the table. Limit butter to small amounts, and choose low-fat or nonfat versions of dairy products to avoid too much saturated fat. Fatty fish (such as salmon and tuna), walnuts, and canola oil all provide omega-3 fatty acids, essential fats that our bodies cannot make and that are good for cardiovascular health.

Stay hydrated. You may have heard the conventional wisdom to drink eight glasses of water a day. In reality, you don't need to drink that much, but it's important to drink fluids to avoid getting dehydrated, which can affect your energy levels and cause constipation, headaches, and dizziness. Choose low- or no-calorie liquids like water or seltzer, coffee, and tea, and avoid sugary drinks. Low-fat or skim milk and 100% juice can also be part of your diet, but limit them to small glasses because of the higher calories. Beverages aren't the only way to hydrate. You actually get quite a lot of water from the foods you eat, such as fruits, vegetables, or low-sodium soups.

Go easy on alcohol. Though a drink a day may be good for your heart, drinking too much harms health in many ways, from contributing to automobile accidents to making bones more likely to break. It also makes you unsteady on your feet and more prone to falls, injuries, and accidents.

Do you need supplements?

It's best to get nutrients from the foods you eat and not from supplements. That said, taking a daily multivitamin is a reasonable step for filling gaps in nutrition. Choose a supplement that gives you the standard recommended daily doses of vitamins and minerals. Avoid those that offer "super" doses of any nutrient. Three specific supplements you might want to ask your doctor about are calcium, vitamin D, and vitamin B_{12}.

Getting a little extra vitamin D—1,000 to 2,000 IU a day—seems to be good for health. Vitamin D deficiency is very common, especially among older adults and people who don't get much sunlight. Extra vitamin D is good for bone health because it helps the body absorb calcium from the food you eat.

The amount of calcium you should get daily rises with age. Men under age 70 and women under age 50 should get 1,000 mg of calcium a day. After that, aim for 1,200 mg a day. Calcium-rich foods include milk and other dairy products and green leafy vegetables. Calcium is often added to cereals, soy milk, breads, and snacks.

Vitamin B_{12} is another vitamin that can be hard to get from food. It's vital for nerve function, but the body's ability to absorb it from food declines over time.

Check with your doctor about which supplements are right for you. He or she can perform simple blood tests to determine whether your levels of vitamin D and vitamin B_{12} are too low.

What's a healthy weight?

As you get older, your metabolism slows down, and you need to eat less and exercise more to maintain the same weight. That's a problem, because weight gain can have serious consequences for mobility. Being overweight or obese can make it difficult for you to rise from a chair, walk around the block, or climb stairs.

Two tools can help you check and monitor your own weight: body mass index (BMI) and waist circumference. BMI is a ratio of weight to height. Health care providers use it to determine whether a person's weight falls within a healthy range. To figure out your BMI, use the online calculator at www.health.harvard.edu/BMI.

A healthy BMI is 19 to 24 in men and 18 to 24 in women. BMIs of 25 to 29 are in the overweight category, while BMIs of 30 or higher are considered obese.

BMI is an imperfect tool. For example, it doesn't capture how much of your body is muscle versus fat. Your doctor can help you assess your body composition and specific disease risks.

Another tool is your waist circumference, or how big your belly is. Why the waist rather than the hips or thighs? Because fat stored in the abdomen around your organs—also called visceral fat—is associated with a higher risk of cardiovascular disease and diabetes. A waist circumference of 35 inches (women) or 40 inches (men) or larger is generally considered a sign of excess visceral fat. Again, these numbers are imperfect because your overall body size might be smaller or larger than others. But measuring your waist is a great way of tracking your health over time and catching any gain in visceral fat before it gets out of control. If you have trouble remembering to measure, use a pair of snug, nonstretchy pants without an elastic waist as a guide—if you find them getting tight, it's a sign to check whether you've gained weight.

Losing weight effectively

Unlike the age-related health problems we've discussed already, obesity can begin to limit mobility early in life. That's a problem, because if you begin to lose your ability to move easily in your 30s or 40s, your chance of remaining healthy and independent in late life fall dramatically. Controlling your weight is important at every age. And the most successful way to do that is through a combination of diet and physical activity.

Daily aerobic activities, like brisk walking, jogging, or other activities that make your heart beat faster, are best for helping you maintain a healthy weight. But in recent years, studies have found that even low-level activities such as standing, pacing, and fidgeting can help you burn as much as 350 additional calories a day. Simply standing burns off three times more calories than sitting. Another helpful aid is a minicycle that you can place in front of your armchair and use while you watch TV.

If possible, add some strength training to your routine—the added muscle will help you rev up your metabolism. If you have a setback like arthritis or a joint replacement, work with your doctor or physical therapist to find an exercise routine you can manage; many people gain weight during illnesses and recoveries and find it hard to get the weight off.

It's hard to lose weight just by exercising. Most people also need to rein in how much they eat. For every pound you'd like to lose, there needs to be a deficit of roughly 3,500 calories. To lose a pound a week, you could eat 500 fewer calories a day, but for most people, that's too drastic a reduction to be sustainable. Instead, try burning 250 extra calories a day through physical activity and eating 250 fewer calories a day.

For weight loss, concentrate on foods that are nutrient-dense but low in calories, such as fruits, vegetables, and beans. These foods are bulky, so they help you feel fuller with fewer calories. You can also trick your mind by buying smaller plates, so portions seem larger, and rearranging your cupboards, so less healthy snacks are harder to reach. And always try to savor your food, really paying attention to its flavors, so you are satisfied with less. ▼

Maintaining independence

Say you're taking all the right steps to make sure that you remain mobile. But does your home—and your larger environment—help or hinder your efforts to maintain independence? There may be ways you can change things to aid your mobility and prevent injuries. You can also be proactive about planning for a future when your mobility may be limited by age or a chronic health problem.

This report has focused on ways to stay healthy and active so that you have the best possible chances of retaining your mobility and independence. But when something does change—a health problem, or increased frailty with aging—some people feel resistant to making changes in their home, their environment, or their routine. They feel that installing bars in the shower or hiring a part-time caregiver is a sign of old age and signals a loss of independence. They keep doing things the same way even if that way is harder and they are putting their own safety at risk.

It's important to keep the bigger goal in mind. If standing in the shower is difficult for you, install a shower seat so you won't fall and break a hip. If you have a health problem that makes shopping at the grocery store painful, have groceries delivered rather than sacrificing a healthy, balanced diet. If you are concerned about driving, maybe there are adaptations you can make (see "Driving: Staying up to the challenge," page 33). Knowing how to set priorities for your health and adapt your environment as needed will help you stay healthy.

Aging in place

Most people would rather stay in their homes as they grow older instead of mov-ing to a retirement community or nursing home. The Centers for Disease Control and Prevention defines "aging in place" as the ability to live in one's own home and community safely, independently, and comfortably, regardless of age, income, or ability level.

Lately there has been a surge of interest in research, policies, and design that contribute to the goal of aging in place. Cities and communities are beginning to pay more attention to designing age-friendly streets and public spaces. And a growing number of services are available to help older people modify their own homes to make life easier.

Aging in place isn't about avoiding change. It's about making adaptations to your existing home and lifestyle as you age. Even if you stay in your own home, you should expect to make at least some changes in your home's design or furnishings to accommodate changing physical abilities, as well as modifying some of your routines around the house. Some people are designing and remodeling homes based on universal design principles, which have features that allow a home to accommodate people of varying ages and abilities.

Adapting and fall-proofing your home

Improving your balance, strength, and coordination is a great way to prevent falls. But tripping hazards at home also pose a risk. You should periodically make a safety inventory of your home to eliminate fall dangers.

Over time, you may need to make larger adjustments to your home's design or move to a home that is easier to navigate and maintain. There's a burgeoning industry

Keeping in touch with friends and socializing regularly can help ward off depression and give you the mental boost you need to take care of yourself properly.

to help people age in place: the National Association of Home Builders, for instance, now offers a training program for certified aging-in-place specialists who focus on refitting homes for older adults. Don't automatically assume you need extensive remodeling; focus modifications on what suits your needs and lifestyle. You can also invest in emergency response systems that give you an added measure of security (see "Technology to keep tabs on you," page 46).

Throughout the home

- Use flooring that is smooth, nonglare, and slip-resistant. A slippery floor is a fall waiting to happen. Also, carpets and rugs should have a pile that's less than half an inch deep, and rugs should have nonskid pads or backings to keep them from sliding or folding over. Keep floors clear of clutter that someone could trip on.
- Keep hallways well lit, and put night lights in bedrooms, bathrooms, and connecting hallways.
- Keep electrical cords for floor lamps, TVs, phones, and other devices tucked away from where you walk or against the walls.
- Make sure stairs have a handrail that runs the full length of the stairs and just past them, and a light switch at the top and bottom. For extra safety, install handrails on both sides of staircases.
- Install a high-tech security system that can directly contact police, fire, and emergency medical services.
- If you have a wheelchair, make sure the living area, kitchen, and at least one bedroom and bathroom have a five-foot by five-foot clear space for accommodating wheelchair movements. The main bedroom, a full bath, and living areas should be on a single floor, with no stairs separating rooms or areas. Hallways should be at least 36 inches wide, and windows should be low and easy to open, shut, and lock.

House exterior

- For general safety, install lighting at doorways, porches, and walkways. Motion detector lights are best for lighting the way when you come home at night.

- If you live in an area that gets snow, keep supplies like shovels and melting salt handy, and consider paying for a service to clear walkways of snow and ice if it's difficult for you.
- Keep walkways in good repair, with an even surface. Uneven pavement is easy to trip on.
- If you're moving to a new house, choose one with a low-maintenance exterior, such as vinyl or brick.
- Landscape with low-maintenance shrubs and plants.

Entrances and doors

- Make sure you have at least one no-step entrance, lit with a sensor light.
- Fix doors to the house so they are easy to unlock and open. If it takes you a while to turn a key, install a keyless entry using a card or remote control. If grip strength is a problem for you, install handles instead of doorknobs. Some companies sell levers that you can attach to a doorknob to serve the same purpose (see "Helpful devices and products," page 47).
- Doors should be at least 32 inches wide, or preferably 36 inches.
- Remove any doormats or rugs that you might trip on. Raised thresholds can be lowered or ramps installed, if needed.

Bathroom

- Add grab bars (which are sturdier than towel bars) to your shower or bath. Grab bars are also useful near the toilet for getting up and down. The bathroom is one of the most dangerous rooms of the house and a frequent site of injuries and falls.
- Consider adding a bathing stool or shower seat, along with a handheld shower head attached to a hose. These make it easier to bathe sitting down.
- In the tub, install a nonslip surface, or add a nonslip mat. On the floor, consider using textured tiles, which tend to be less slippery when wet.
- A contrasting border on the edge of the bathroom countertop can make it easier to see.
- Consider making at least one bathroom on the main level wheelchair-maneuverable, with a 60-inch turning radius or acceptable T-turn space,

and a clear space that's 36 inches square or 30 inches by 48 inches.

Bedroom

- Rearrange your closet so you can easily reach things you need.
- Take steps to make sure you can get into and out of bed easily and safely. A firm mattress will make it easier, as will a bed that is low enough to the ground that your feet touch the floor when you're sitting on the edge of the bed. Install bedrails to help you raise and lower yourself if needed.
- Put lamps at the bedside that are easy to switch on and off.

Kitchen

- Rearrange cabinets and drawers so you can reach food, dishes, pots, and utensils without straining. Store the heaviest items in places where you don't have to bend down or reach high.
- Keep a sturdy step stool on hand if you have high cabinets that are difficult to reach.
- Install single-lever faucets, which are easier to operate, and counters with rounded corners.

Adapting your lifestyle

In addition to home modifications, you may have to make changes in your lifestyle and routine so that you can remain in your home. Some changes mean paying more for services, but they may be worth the money if they help you avoid an expensive move to an assisted living facility and help you stay in a home you love:

- Ask for help with raking leaves, home repairs, gardening, or snow removal, from either a relative, a neighbor, or a paid service.
- Pay for an occasional housecleaning service to clean areas that are hard for you to reach.
- Hire an in-home caregiver or homemaker to help you with medical tasks or household tasks you can't do on your own.
- Have groceries delivered if you have difficulty accessing fresh, healthy foods on your own regularly.
- Make an effort to be in better contact with neigh-

bors and with nearby relatives and friends; try to establish regular check-ins, particularly if you are dealing with health issues.

Choosing services

What type of assistance do you need to be able to stay in your home? Here are some options.

Hired companions and homemakers. You may want to hire someone to help with meals, shopping, and laundry. Sometimes an informal arrangement—such as a college student who lives in a home and provides help in exchange for rent—works well.

Meal programs. Hot, nutritious meals may be available through programs like the Meals on Wheels Association of America (www.mowaa.org) or Eating Together, which offers lunch and companionship at community centers, sometimes with transportation. Senior centers, community groups, or religious organizations may have similar services.

Transportation services. Some communities offer free or low-cost transportation to medical appointments for seniors or people who are disabled. Other good sources of free or low-cost assistance are religious and community organizations, such as churches or synagogues, councils on aging, and senior centers.

Finding help

The U.S. Department of Health and Human Services has an Eldercare Locator that connects you to services available in your area, including financial assistance, transportation, long-term care, and volunteer services. See http://eldercare.gov or call 800-677-1116.

BenefitsCheckUp, a service of the National Council on Aging, connects people 55 or older to hundreds of benefits that cover some costs for rent, property taxes, heating and utility bills, health care, prescription drugs, and other services or goods. You can choose to use the full benefits database or one that focuses only on prescription drug coverage. You can use these free services as often as you like. The questionnaire at www.benefitscheckup.org takes less than half an hour to fill out. It requires personal financial information, but it is confidential. If you appear to qualify for any programs, the service gives you contact information so you can request the benefit. Internet access and computer skills are necessary to fill out the forms.

In addition, the United Way can help you locate resources in your area.

Assessing your community

The design of a community can affect the mobility of its residents. You may not have much control over how your neighborhood or city is designed, but it's good to be aware of how your environment affects your mobility. You can advocate for changes that will improve mobility in your community, whether it involves bringing the issue to your condo or neighborhood association, your city councilor, or your state representative. This awareness can also guide any decision you make about whether to move, and where. Every neighborhood comes with trade-offs—you may prefer to live close to a family member, for instance, even if it's far from grocery stores. But taking an inventory of how your neighborhood meets your needs can help you find ways to work around the challenges.

Public transportation. Most people outlive their ability to drive. Yet some communities that cater to retirees are far from urban areas with robust public transit systems. And many centers that offer affordable housing and services to older adults are often located in suburbs inconvenient to shopping centers and grocery stores. While these places are attractive because they offer quiet, peaceful living "away from it all," they become much more isolating if you can't drive, or if driving is challenging for you. Having access to reliable public transportation could allow you to remain independent and active as you age. Some communities offer special shuttles or dial-a-ride services to seniors and people with disabilities who have trouble getting to transit stops and stations, or who need transport to major medical centers for treatment.

Driveability. How easy is it to drive in your community? If you are in an area that's frequently affected by snowstorms, is there a reliable plowing service? Are streets well marked, and can you park easily at grocery stores, medical centers, and other places you frequent?

Walkability. Living in a walkable neighborhood can vastly improve your health and mobility by encouraging you to use your body to get around rather than driving. Even if you regularly go to a gym or work out at home, the ability to easily and safely walk to a grocery store or do other errands on foot will add to your daily activity level. A walkable neighbor-

Technology to keep tabs on you

Do you worry that you may fall and be unable to summon help, or that you may accidentally leave your stove on or forget to take your medications? A variety of technologies are now available that can help.

Most people are familiar with the emergency response system known as Lifeline, thanks to its well-known commercial (with the woman who cries, "I've fallen and I can't get up!"). About 12% of care recipients have such a system, according to a National Alliance for Caregiving survey. About the same percentage rely on a device that sends information electronically to a doctor or care manager, and one in 10 uses sensors in the home that can detect problems such as when the person falls, wanders away, or leaves the stove on.

Some experts refer to such devices and systems as "telecare." People can use body sensors that measure vital signs like heart rate and blood pressure, and a noninvasive (needle-free) technique to measure blood sugar levels is under development. Other home sensors include devices on beds and refrigerators to help determine if and when you are sleeping and eating, for example. Still other devices dispense medications at predetermined times and give reminders to take the pills.

This trend is even extending to home design. The Environmental Geriatrics program at Weill Cornell Medical College (www.environmentalgeriatrics.com) focuses on the design and application of specialized features to create home interiors and products that keep seniors healthy and functioning well on their own.

Cellphones can also serve a role in telecare in a variety of ways, such as storing and transmitting vital signs, providing reminders when a measurement or medication is due, or (in phones with a global positioning device or GPS) serving as a tracking device if a person wanders away.

If you feel such technology could be helpful for yourself or your loved one, a number of companies provide telecare systems. Your geriatric care manager or doctor may also be a resource for finding an appropriate system.

hood generally has dedicated sidewalks and marked crossings for pedestrians, and shops, parks, and other destinations within walking distance.

Safety. How older adults perceive the safety of their neighborhoods shapes their health. One survey of 18,000 people over age 50 found that those who perceived their neighborhoods were unsafe were more likely to experience functional decline over a 10-year period and were less likely to recover from mobility problems. Perceptions don't always match reality, of course, so although in some cases the problem is the neighborhood itself, in other cases the solution might be to improve a person's sense of personal safety.

Access to shops and services. Access to grocery stores with fresh food is important for maintaining a healthy lifestyle and also for preserving independence with aging. So is access to pharmacies, clinics, and any other services you depend on for your health.

Social environment. Do you have relatives or friends who live near you and whom you visit regularly? Are there places where you can socialize and meet other people, like community centers, fitness centers, or clubs? Are there any neighborhood social activities? Some people pursue retirement dreams that involve moving to warm places where they have always wanted to live, only to find they are more isolated from family and friends.

Seeing a geriatrician

Good medical planning is essential to maintaining independence. One cornerstone of good medical care is an experienced, approachable primary care doctor who can coordinate your care and help you interact with specialists as needed.

It's not unusual to see the same doctor for decades. But in old age, it's wise to consider switching to a geriatrician or at least consulting one. Geriatricians have expertise in dealing with many chronic conditions—such as heart ailments, high blood pressure, diabetes, and disabilities—common in older adults. They are trained to consider the needs of the whole person and focus on function and quality of life. Some geriatricians routinely make home visits to see how you live and what changes could improve safety, nutri-

> ### ▶ Helpful devices and products
>
> A number of companies offer an array of devices and products that can help you depend less on assistance from others, from canes and walkers to easy-to-use household gadgets like book magnifiers and jar openers. Here are two online companies, which also offer printed catalogs.
>
> **Assisted Living Store, Inc.**
> 199 Bridgepoint Drive
> South St. Paul, MN 55075
> 888-388-5862 (toll-free)
> www.assistedlivingstore.com
>
> **Independent Living Aids**
> P.O. Box 9022
> Hicksville, NY 11802
> 800-537-2118 (toll-free)
> www.independentliving.com

tion, function, and mobility. Usually, they recognize the importance of allowing family members to attend appointments.

Geriatricians are also well aware of the harmful effects that medications can have on older people. It's common for older people to be given prescriptions for several medications, because they often have numerous health problems. The more medications a person takes, the higher the risk of drug interactions and harmful side effects. Older people are especially vulnerable because of age-related changes in body composition. They have less muscle mass and their bodies process drugs differently than younger people's do. Even over-the-counter medications can contribute to this problem, and the effects can be cumulative. Roughly one-third of older people experience harmful drug side effects each year. And these adverse effects are responsible for nearly one-third of hospital admissions in the elderly. It's essential to keep tabs on possible drug interactions and to calibrate pain medications carefully.

A comprehensive geriatric evaluation can offer wide-ranging advice that vastly improves your quality of life and ability to live independently. That might include recommendations to change or discard medications, consult with a physical therapist or occupational therapist, adapt the home, pursue neuropsychological testing, or add home care services. Medicare or Medicaid will pay for the evaluation. Some private insurance plans also provide coverage if the primary care physician makes a referral.

Making a move

There are many more options than there used to be for living arrangements. Your goal of independent living may be to stay in your own home, but many people find that there's also a freedom in having more help and resources available, which lets them be more healthy and active. What's important is that you make a plan based on your own values and priorities, rather than making rushed decisions when a sudden medical setback like a broken hip or stroke makes it necessary.

Retirement communities. Many communities have been designed specifically for seniors, and with the baby boomer generation aging, new kinds of niche communities have emerged. Some are based around shared pursuits, like fitness or arts and crafts. Some communities are linked to universities and provide opportunities to take classes and attend cultural events. In addition to connecting you with like-minded people, these communities offer helpful resources (like lawn care and snow removal), security systems, and opportunities for social interaction.

NORCs. A naturally occurring retirement community (NORC) is another option. These neighborhoods and complexes house people at a range of different ages, but because they have coordinated care and support available, they are senior-friendly. Several communities in the United States have received grants from the U.S. Administration on Aging to fund local NORCs. Your local agency on aging may have information on what is available in your area.

"Granny pods." Think of these structures, also called accessory dwelling units, as a more private version of an in-law apartment. A granny pod is a small, prefabricated cottage built in the backyard of one of your adult children. You have privacy, but you can easily visit your children and grandkids—and in the case of an emergency, those who care about you are close at hand. Some models—like the MEDCottage designed by the company N2CARE—can include equipment to monitor medical conditions and provide added security (see "Technology to keep tabs on you," page 46).

Continuing care communities. These are similar to retirement communities but have medical staff and facilities on site, so that a person can move from a home to an assisted living unit or nursing bed easily if he or she becomes ill. If you move to this kind of community, make sure you are comfortable with the setup of each level of care. The communities often require a high entrance fee as a prepayment for later care, as well as a monthly fee. Make sure the facility has a good track record and is likely to continue to thrive, and that the fee structure makes financial sense to you.

Assisted living. People who can't live on their own because they need help with everyday tasks such as bathing, dressing, making meals, and doing laundry may consider an assisted living facility. This option does not provide round-the-clock nursing care, but many assisted living facilities have nursing homes nearby, so in case needs change, residents can transfer to another location. Assisted living can cost around $25,000 to $50,000 per year, and is often covered by long-term care insurance but not private medical insurance or Medicare.

Nursing homes. A nursing home is the most comprehensive level of care for people who are too sick to live alone or to be cared for at home. Some basically look like a hospital, while others are designed to look more like houses or feel more like a home. Nursing homes are also the most expensive living situation, costing on average about $80,000 a year, though facilities differ widely in costs.

The importance of socializing

One measure of successful independence is easy to overlook—staying in touch with friends and family. As you retire, you may start to lose your sense of belonging in the community. But social engagements—or even regular phone calls with family and friends—can help you maintain your contacts and feel more engaged with the world. They can help keep you on top of current events. And they can just make you happier. We are social beings, and remaining so is good for mental and physical health. Socializing can help you ward off depression and other mental problems. Moreover, the lift you get from seeing friends can give you the energy you need to care for yourself properly, to eat right, to engage in physical activity—to do all the things that will help you remain mobile and independent for many years to come. ◆

Resources

Organizations

American Academy of Physical Medicine and Rehabilitation
9700 W. Bryn Mawr Ave., Suite 200
Rosemont, IL 60018
847-737-6000
www.aapmr.org

This national organization is for doctors who specialize in physical medicine and rehabilitation for musculoskeletal and neurological problems. AAPMR offers referrals to these doctors and information on a variety of conditions such as low back and neck pain, spinal cord and brain injuries, osteoporosis, and arthritis.

American Physical Therapy Association
1111 N. Fairfax St.
Alexandria, VA 22314
800-999-2782 (toll-free)
www.apta.org

This national professional organization fosters advances in education, research, and the practice of physical therapy. The website has a search engine to help locate board-certified clinical specialists who have additional training in specific areas of physical therapy.

Arthritis Foundation
1330 W. Peachtree St., Suite 100
Atlanta, GA 30309
800-283-7800 (toll-free)
www.arthritis.org

This nonprofit foundation sponsors public education programs and continuing education for professionals, raises money for research, and publishes patient information materials. Local chapters can advise about doctors and sponsor activities such as swimming and self-help classes.

National Council on Aging
1901 L St. NW, 4th Floor
Washington, DC 20036
202-479-1200
www.ncoa.org

This nonprofit service and advocacy organization represents older adults and the community organizations that serve them. The website offers information on fall prevention programs and other health resources for seniors.

National Institute on Aging
Building 31, Room 5C27
31 Center Drive, MSC 2292
Bethesda, MD 20892
800-222-2225 (toll-free) TTY: 800-222-4225 (toll-free)
www.nia.nih.gov

This branch of the National Institutes of Health offers reliable, free information on aging-related health issues.

Publications

This report draws on information from the following Special Health Reports from Harvard Medical School. If you want to find out more about a particular topic, you can order these reports online at www.health.harvard.edu or by calling 877-649-9457 (toll-free).

The Aging Eye
Laura C. Fine, M.D., and Jeffrey S. Heier, M.D., Medical Editors
(Harvard Medical School, 2012)

Back Pain: Healing Your Aching Back
Jeffrey N. Katz, M.D., Medical Editor
(Harvard Medical School, 2014)

Better Balance: Easy Exercises to Improve Stability and Prevent Falls
Suzanne Salamon, M.D., and Brad Manor, Ph.D., Medical Editors
With Josie Gardiner and Joy Prouty, Master Trainers
(Harvard Medical School, 2012)

Gentle Core Exercises: Start Toning Your Abs, Building Your Back Muscles, and Reclaiming Core Fitness Today
Edward M. Phillips, M.D., Medical Editor
Josie Gardiner, Master Trainer and Fitness Consultant
(Harvard Medical School, 2013)

Hearing Loss: A Guide to Prevention and Treatment
David Murray Vernick, M.D., and Ann Gentili-Stockwell, M.A., Medical Editors
(Harvard Medical School, 2013)

The Joint Pain Relief Workout: Healing Exercises for Your Shoulders, Hips, Knees, and Ankles
Edward M. Phillips, M.D., Medical Editor
With Josie Gardiner and Joy Prouty, Master Trainers
(Harvard Medical School, 2012)

Knees and Hips: A Troubleshooting Guide to Knee and Hip Pain
Scott D. Martin, M.D., Medical Editor
(Harvard Medical School, 2012)

Living Well with Osteoarthritis: A Guide to Keeping Your Joints Healthy
Robert H. Shmerling, M.D., Medical Editor
(Harvard Medical School, 2013)

Osteoporosis: A Guide to Prevention and Treatment
David M. Slovik, M.D., Medical Editor
(Harvard Medical School, 2013)

Strength and Power Training: A Guide for Older Adults
Julie K. Silver, M.D., Medical Editor
(Harvard Medical School, 2013)

Harvard Health Publications
Trusted advice for a healthier life

 Receive *HEALTHbeat*, Harvard Health Publications' free email newsletter

Go to: **www.health.harvard.edu** to subscribe to *HEALTHbeat*.

This free weekly email newsletter brings you health tips, advice, and information on a wide range of topics.

You can also join in discussion with experts from Harvard Health Publications and folks like you on a variety of health topics, medical news, and views by reading the Harvard Health Blog (**www.health.harvard.edu/blog**).

Order this report and other publications from Harvard Medical School

online | **www.health.harvard.edu**

phone | **877-649-9457 (toll-free)**

mail | **Belvoir Media Group**
Attn: Harvard Health Publications
P.O. Box 5656
Norwalk, CT 06856-5656

bulk rate | **licensing@belvoir.com**

www.health.harvard.edu
877-649-9457 (toll free)

Other publications from Harvard Medical School

Special Health Reports *Harvard Medical School publishes in-depth reports on a wide range of health topics, including:*

Addiction	Eye Disease	Pain Relief
Aging Successfully	Foot Care	Positive Psychology
Alcohol	Grief & Loss	Prostate Disease
Allergies	Hands	Reducing Sugar & Salt
Alzheimer's Disease	Headache	Sensitive Gut
Anxiety & Phobias	Hearing Loss	Sexuality
Back Pain	Heart Disease	Six-Week Eating Plan
Balance	Heart Disease & Diet	Skin Care
Caregivers	High Blood Pressure	Sleep
Change Made Easy	Incontinence	Strength Training
Cholesterol	Knees & Hips	Stress Management
Core Exercises	Living Wills	Stroke
Depression	Memory	Thyroid Disease
Diabetes	Men's Health	Vitamins & Minerals
Diabetes & Diet	Mobility/Independence	Weight Loss
Energy/Fatigue	Neck Pain	Women's Health
Erectile Dysfunction	Nutrition	Workout Workbook
Exercise	Osteoarthritis	
Exercise Your Joints	Osteoporosis	

Periodicals *Monthly newsletters and annual publications, including:*

Harvard Health Letter	*Harvard Heart Letter*	*Prostate Disease Annual*
Harvard Women's Health Watch	*Harvard Men's Health Watch*	

ISBN 978-1-61401-067-8

99500

9 781614 010678

ISBN 978-1-61401-067-8
SV99500

MI0414